Living Clojure

Carin Meier

Beijing · Boston · Farnham · Sebastopol · Tokyo

Living Clojure

by Carin Meier

Printed in the United States of America.

Published by O'Reilly Media, Inc., 1005 Gravenstein Highway North, Sebastopol, CA 95472.

O'Reilly books may be purchased for educational, business, or sales promotional use. Online editions are also available for most titles (*http://safaribooksonline.com*). For more information, contact our corporate/institutional sales department: 800-998-9938 or *corporate@oreilly.com*.

Editor: Meghan Blanchette	**Indexer:** WordCo Indexing Services, Inc.
Production Editor: Matthew Hacker	**Interior Designer:** David Futato
Copyeditor: Kim Cofer	**Cover Designer:** Ellie Volckhausen
Proofreader: Jasmine Kwityn	**Illustrator:** Rebecca Demarest

April 2015: First Edition

Revision History for the First Edition

2015-04-09: First Release
2016-02-05: Second Release

See *http://oreilly.com/catalog/errata.csp?isbn=9781491909041* for release details.

978-1-491-90904-1

[LSI]

Table of Contents

Part II. Living Clojure Training Program

Dedicated to Jim Weirich (1956–2014), whose love of life and learning inspired so many.

Preface

The inspiration for this book comes from two things. The first and most direct one is from my years of learning, exploring, and finally working professionally in Clojure. The second, more indirect one, is from my experience of taking up running for the first time. My first attempt on my own was an utter failure. I thought that maybe I just wasn't cut out to run. Luckily, I was introduced to a great program called Couch to 5k. The creators of the app realized that the most common reason people failed to achieve their fitness goals was because they were trying to do too much, too fast. To solve this problem, a gradual, 8-week training program was developed to help users achieve the goal of running for 30 minutes without stopping. Although it wasn't easy, I managed to successfully complete the program and could run for a 30-minute stretch.

A few weeks later, I was with a group of fellow developers after attending a community user group. The conversation turned to Clojure. A few of us were discussing how much we enjoyed using the language, although one of our friends complained how he had tried to learn Clojure, but just couldn't get it. I found out that he had tried to cram in learning it all in one weekend. Too much, too soon. The problems of learning how to run did not seem that much different from the problem of learning a new language. The process of learning a new language also involves learning a new way to think—training the brain to process inputs and solve problems in a new way. This doesn't happen overnight. It comes, like training for running, after building up with practice.

This book combines these inspirations. The result is both a primer on learning Clojure and a structured training program to build up your brain to think a new way.

Who This Book Is For

Are you looking for a gentle introduction to Clojure? Do you already have a background in another programming language? Perfect! This book is for you. We will be covering programming concepts as they relate to Clojure and its unique design. We will also touch on object-oriented programming and concepts in comparison to functional programming. In the dicussion, we will be assuming familiarity with object-oriented development. So, if you are coming from another language like Ruby or Java, you should feel right at home. If you are a newer programmer, this book will be best paired with a more general introduction or reference to programming concepts.

If you are a language expert, or want a deep dive into every nook and cranny of Clojure, this book is most likely not for you. We will be concentrating on the major aspects of the language, not the minutiae, with the goal being to learn how to *think* Clojure. The same philosophy goes for tools and libraries in the Clojure ecosystem. We are striving for a primer that will present an overall holistic view of the most common and pragmatic parts, so that after finishing the book you will be comfortable and ready to start *living* Clojure.

How to Use This Book

The structure of this book is built around training with knowledge and practice to live Clojure. Just like the inspirations for it, it is composed of two main parts. Part I is a tour of the simplicity and power of the Clojure programming language. It will cover useful libraries and common uses of Clojure. Part II is the *Living Clojure* Training Program. It will take you through a weekly training program designed to give you the practice, knowledge, and tools you need to get up and running and thriving as a Clojure developer.

The first half of the book will introduce the language, along with some code examples. There are a few important things to keep in mind, as outlined in the following subsections.

Do Try the Examples

I know it is tempting to read through the book as fast as possible. But actually typing in the code examples and seeing the magic for yourself will help your understanding grow. Take the time to try out the new concepts and commands for yourself. We will be walking through setting up your environment to run Clojure later in this Preface.

Don't Feel Overwhelmed

We are going to cover a lot of material during the first half of the book. It is not all going to sink in right away. That is perfectly fine! In fact, this book was designed for that. The second half of the book is a training program that builds on the overview so that the basic language concepts really sink in with use. Once you start the training program, and questions start to come up, you will have all the tools and general knowledge to know where to look for the solutions.

Again, it takes time to learn to think in a new way. Be patient.

Don't Worry About the Parens

A common initial concern from people looking at Clojure is about the parentheses.

Don't worry about the parens.

Really.

After you get into Clojure with a good editor that supports a *paredit mode*—that is, a mode that always inserts the matching parens for you—they will seem to disappear. We will cover choosing and setting up an editor later on in Chapter 4.

The simplicity and elegance that the parens structure gives to Clojure is one of its main advantages. In fact, some people even come to think of the parens as a hug for their code.

One More Thing—Have Fun!

Clojure is a delightful language to use. Learning a new language is an exciting adventure, full of wonder. Embrace it.

Code examples can sometimes be stodgy, dry, full of meaningless numbers, and quite frankly, boring. This book strives to fight against this by using the power of storytelling to strengthen the code examples. Our brains become more active during stories. In fact, studies have shown that learning actually increases when problems are presented through a narrative. Thus, we are going to call upon a famous story to accompany us through this book: *Alice in Wonderland* by Lewis Carroll.

As you explore Clojure, the story of *Alice in Wonderland* will be woven through the code examples as well. Her adventures will remind you to relax, smile, and have fun on your journey.

What You Need to Use This Book

Before starting a journey, we need to pack our suitcases and prepare. Luckily, there is not much we need to get started on our adventure.

Install Java

If your computer doesn't already have Java installed on it, you will need to get it. You can check to see if it is already set up by opening a command prompt and typing:

```
java -version
```

You should see something that looks like this:

```
java version "1.7.0_60"
Java(TM) SE Runtime Environment (build 1.7.0_60-b19)
Java HotSpot(TM) 64-Bit Server VM (build 24.60-b09, mixed mode)
```

If you see a version that is 1.6 or greater, you are ready to go. If not, you can download the latest version from the Java site (*http://bit.ly/java_se_versions*).

 Wait. Why do I need Java? I want to learn Clojure.

Clojure runs on the Java virtual machine (JVM), which is a mature and robust platform used by many large enterprises. It is a great environment for running fast, scalable, and dependable programs.

You don't *need* to know Java to write Clojure code. However, you can use and interact with Java classes and libraries if you want to. You'll learn how to do this after we explore the language a bit first.

Now that you have Java installed, there is only one more thing you need before you are ready: a Clojure REPL.

Getting Your Clojure REPL Ready

Clojure has an important interactive tool called the REPL, which stands for read-eval-print loop. Once you get into the Clojure REPL, you are right there in the language. You will be able to enter Clojure code, hit Return, and the REPL will evaluate and print out the result for you. It is your key for exploring the language.

Let's try out a Clojure REPL right now. We will be using the REPL all through the book to try out and explore code. In the early chapters, we will be exclusively trying out code in the REPL. As we move into creating projects with Clojure in Chapter 4, we will cover different editors and tooling. Right now, we are going to use the easiest way to try out a REPL, using *Leiningen*, a popular tool for creating Clojure projects.

Follow these steps to get a REPL up and running:

1. Visit the Leiningen website (*http://leiningen.org*) and follow the instructions to download.

2. Create a new project called *wonderland* with the following command:

    ```
    -> lein new wonderland
    ```

3. Go into the newly created project with this command:

    ```
    -> cd wonderland
    ```

4. Run the following command to start up the Clojure REPL:

    ```
    -> lein repl
    ```

You will see the following:

```
nREPL server started on port 65247 on host 127.0.0.1 - nrepl://127.0.0.1:65247
REPL-y 0.3.1
Clojure 1.6.0
    Docs: (doc function-name-here)
          (find-doc "part-of-name-here")
  Source: (source function-name-here)
 Javadoc: (javadoc java-object-or-class-here)
    Exit: Control+D or (exit) or (quit)
 Results: Stored in vars *1, *2, *3, an exception in *e

user=>
```

The final line is the REPL prompt waiting for your input. Try typing in the following and pressing Return:

```
(+ 1 1)
```

You should see a 2 appear on the next line as the result:

```
nREPL server started on port 65361 on host 127.0.0.1 - nrepl://127.0.0.1:65361
REPL-y 0.3.1
Clojure 1.6.0
    Docs: (doc function-name-here)
          (find-doc "part-of-name-here")
  Source: (source function-name-here)
 Javadoc: (javadoc java-object-or-class-here)
    Exit: Control+D or (exit) or (quit)
 Results: Stored in vars *1, *2, *3, an exception in *e

user=> (+ 1 1)
2
user=>
```

The REPL just *read* in what you typed, *evaluated* it, and *printed* out the result for you.

Throughout the book, this is how we will structure the code, and the return values for the code will be shown with two semicolons followed by an arrow, like this:

```
(+ 1 1)
;; -> 2
```

The semicolon signifies a comment in Clojure. When it comes time to evaluate the code, everything after the semicolon on that line is ignored. If you are using an electronic version of this book, this makes it convenient to copy and paste whole examples very easily into your REPL and try them out for yourself.

You now hold the power of the REPL in your hands. We'll begin our journey to explore Clojure with it in Chapter 1.

Conventions Used in This Book

The following typographical conventions are used in this book:

Italic
> Indicates new terms, URLs, email addresses, filenames, and file extensions.

`Constant width`
> Used for program listings, as well as within paragraphs to refer to program elements such as variable or function names, databases, data types, environment variables, statements, and keywords.

`Constant width bold`
> Shows commands or other text that should be typed literally by the user.

`Constant width italic`
> Shows text that should be replaced with user-supplied values or by values determined by context.

 This element signifies a tip or suggestion.

 This element signifies a general note.

 This element indicates a warning or caution.

Using Code Examples

Supplemental material (code examples, exercises, etc.) is available for download at *https://github.com/gigasquid/wonderland-clojure-katas*.

This book is here to help you get your job done. In general, if example code is offered with this book, you may use it in your programs and documentation. You do not need to contact us for permission unless you're reproducing a significant portion of the code. For example, writing a program that uses several chunks of code from this book does not require permission. Selling or distributing a CD-ROM of examples from O'Reilly books does require permission. Answering a question by citing this book and quoting example code does not require permission. Incorporating a significant amount of example code from this book into your product's documentation does require permission.

We appreciate, but do not require, attribution. An attribution usually includes the title, author, publisher, and ISBN. For example: "*Living Clojure* by Carin Meier (O'Reilly). Copyright 2015 Carin Meier, 978-1-491-90904-1."

If you feel your use of code examples falls outside fair use or the permission given above, feel free to contact us at *permissions@oreilly.com*.

Safari® Books Online

 *Safari Books Online* is an on-demand digital library that delivers expert content in both book and video form from the world's leading authors in technology and business.

Technology professionals, software developers, web designers, and business and creative professionals use Safari Books Online as their primary resource for research, problem solving, learning, and certification training.

Safari Books Online offers a range of plans and pricing for enterprise, government, education, and individuals.

Members have access to thousands of books, training videos, and prepublication manuscripts in one fully searchable database from publishers like O'Reilly Media, Prentice Hall Professional, Addison-Wesley Professional, Microsoft Press, Sams, Que, Peachpit Press, Focal Press, Cisco Press, John Wiley & Sons, Syngress, Morgan Kaufmann, IBM Redbooks, Packt, Adobe Press, FT Press, Apress, Manning, New Riders, McGraw-Hill, Jones & Bartlett, Course Technology, and hundreds more. For more information about Safari Books Online, please visit us online.

How to Contact Us

Please address comments and questions concerning this book to the publisher:

O'Reilly Media, Inc.
1005 Gravenstein Highway North
Sebastopol, CA 95472
800-998-9938 (in the United States or Canada)
707-829-0515 (international or local)
707-829-0104 (fax)

We have a web page for this book, where we list errata, examples, and any additional information. You can access this page at *http://bit.ly/living_clojure*.

To comment or ask technical questions about this book, send email to *bookquestions@oreilly.com*.

For more information about our books, courses, conferences, and news, see our website at *http://www.oreilly.com*.

Find us on Facebook: *http://facebook.com/oreilly*

Follow us on Twitter: *http://twitter.com/oreillymedia*

Watch us on YouTube: *http://www.youtube.com/oreillymedia*

Acknowledgments

Writing a book has been one of the most challenging projects I have ever done. I certainly could not have done it alone. I would like to take a moment to call out thanks for everyone who helped, both directly and indirectly.

First is my editor, Meghan Blanchette. Working with a novice author to guide a book's creation is no simple task. She was patient and encouraging, while always pushing me to express programming concepts clearly and logically. She always has the reader's best interests at heart. Thank you. You are awesome.

To all the book reviewers, your feedback is invaluable. In particular, thanks to Colin Jones, Gabriel Andretta, Elliot Hauser, and Luigi Montanez.

Everyone who helped make this book possible with their contributions and permissions. In particular, Alan Malloy, Alex McNamara, David Byrne, and Anthony Grimes, who made helping out with my first Clojure Open Source project so enjoyable. Also, a special thanks to them for allowing the reproduction of the 4Clojure problems in the training plan in this book. Special thanks as well to Phil Hagelberg, not only for Leiningen and Clojars, but also for the guidance on Chapter 5. And thanks to Michael Klishin, James Reeves, Francesco Bellomi, Zachary Kim, Reid McKenzie, and everyone else for their kind use of screenshots for the book.

The Cincinnati Functional Programmers Group, and in particular, Creighton Kirkendall, Joe Herbers, and Benjamin Kyrlach, who helped me found the group all those years ago. You helped provide a strong community in our hometown for Clojure and other functional languages. I am so glad that I started on this journey with you.

The developer community in Cincinnati. I call you all my friends and am eternally grateful for your support and encouragement. Also, all of the regulars at the Friday morning coffee group, who likewise helped me keep my sanity.

The Clojure community for making it such a great place to grow and learn Clojure. Rich Hickey, Stu Halloway, Justin Gehtland, and all of Cognitect for creating great software. Alex Miller for being a superb guy and bringing the community together with incredible conferences. Michael Fogus and Chris Houser for *The Joy of Clojure*, for my first introduction to Clojure and my continued inspiration. All the many people of the Clojure community: David Nolen, Stuart Sierra, Alex Baranosky, Alan Dipert, Ambrose Bonnaire-Sergeant, Jen Smith, Sam Aaron, Jonathan Graham, Eric Normand, Aaron Brooks, Brenton Ashworth, Luke VanderHart, Bodil Stokke, Bruce Durling, Chas Emerick, Tavis Rudd, Chris Ford, Craig Andera, Michael Nygard, Yodit Stanton, David Pollak, Daniel Higginbotham, Ryan Neufeld, Nada Amin, William Byrd, Anna Pawlicka, Kyle Kingsbury, Zach Tellman, Zack Maril, all my Clojure friends at *Outpace Systems*, and all the other people whose names I missed.

Finally, thanks to my family who put up with me working all those weekends and evenings. I love you madly and I promise it will not be the first part in a trilogy.

PART I

A Guided Tour of Clojure

Welcome to the first half of the book. This section is a gentle guided tour of Clojure. It is designed to get you up and running with a rounded understanding of the language, project setup, and useful libraries. Throughout, we will be using Alice's Adventures in Wonderland as a story guide to accompany our code examples—join in and follow along. It will help prepare and prime your brain for Part II, where you will take what you learn and make it your own in the training program.

Most of all, enjoy yourself and have fun exploring the delightful world of Clojure.

CHAPTER 1

The Structure of Clojure

Hello there. Do you have your Clojure REPL ready? If not, be sure to flip back to the Preface for information on getting it up and running so that you can explore the code examples as we go along in this chapter.

Beginning is always the hardest part. There are so many wonderful parts to Clojure that it is hard to figure out where to begin. When in doubt, always start simple. This chapter is about understanding the basic structure of a Clojure expression. So what is the simplest thing that we can enter into our Clojure REPL as code?

How about an integer?

Let's try it together. Type your favorite integer into your REPL and see what happens:

```
42
;; -> 42
```

Here's a rundown of what's going on here:

1. The number 42 was typed into the REPL and the Enter key was hit.

2. The result of the expression was itself (meaning that it self-evaluated to 42).

3. The result of the expression was printed out. Here, we are showing that it is printed out by using the prefix ; ; →.

In this simplest example, we have seen the basic mechanics of Clojure code evaluation. Clojure code is made up of expressions that are then evaluated to return a result. The simplest of these expressions are those that evaluate to themselves. They are called *simple values* or *literals*.

Baby Steps with Simple Values

We can type other kinds of Clojure code into the REPL that will also evaluate to itself. We have done an integer, so let's try a decimal:

```
12.43
;; -> 12.43
```

What about a ratio?

```
1/3
;; -> 1/3
```

Notice that when it was evaluated, it didn't get changed to a decimal. This is pretty nice, because we don't have to worry about truncation of decimals until we absolutely need to. If the ratio of the two integers can be reduced, it will be, like in this example:

```
4/2
;; -> 2
```

Note that this can only be done with integers. Watch what happens when we try with a decimal:

```
4.0/2
;; -> NumberFormatException Invalid number: 4.0/2
```

If we want to actually do some math, we will need a bigger expression—one with parens. Because we were just doing ratios, let's try to divide 1 by 3:

```
(/ 1 3)
;; -> 1/3
```

Of course, you probably noticed the parens. The other thing that makes this different from other languages is that the operator goes first, followed by the values that you want to divide. This is that basic structure of Clojure code. The function or operator goes first, then the parameters that it needs. Also notice that the result is a ratio value.

In Clojure, the function or operator goes first, followed by the parameters that it needs.

Let's return to our division example and do it again, this time with a decimal:

```
(/ 1 3.0)
;; -> 0.3333333333333333
```

The result here is a decimal because we started out with one of the arguments being a decimal.

Let's take a step back from math and numbers, and talk about some other simple values that evaluate to themselves, like strings. Are you hungry? How about typing **"jam"**, into your REPL?

```
"jam"
;; -> "jam"
```

Strings in Clojure are fun and easy—you just need to put quotes around some text.

Keywords are symbolic identifiers in Clojure whose names start with a colon. They have special properties that make them very useful in ways that we will explain later on. They are simple values, too—try jam as a keyword by putting a colon right in front of the letters:

```
:jam
;; -> :jam
```

Sometimes you don't want to refer to a string or keyword, but want to find a particular letter that someone typed on the keyboard. To do that, you would type the letter preceded by a backslash—for example, to find the letter "j" you would type \j, and Clojure would know you mean the character (or *char*, for short). This is great because if we just want one character, we don't need to have the overhead of an entire string:

```
\j
;; -> \j
```

Let's see. Any other basic simple values that evaluate to themselves? Oh yes, booleans. Let's do `true` and `false` together:

```
true
;; -> true

false
;; -> false
```

There is one more. The small, but important `nil`. It represents the absence of a value in Clojure. Hi, `nil`:

```
nil
;; -> nil
```

We have just seen simple values in Clojure. We can now *do* something with them. One of the things that we can do with them is to use them in expressions. We have already done this with some simple divison. Here is another example with addition:

```
(+ 1 1)
;; -> 2
```

The expression evaluated to a result that is a value of 2.

These expressions can also be nested:

```
(+ 1 (+ 8 3))
;; -> 12
```

In this case, the inner expression of (+ 8 3) was evaluated first and then 1 was added to the result.

We can use simple values in expressions. We can also use these values in other Clojure data collections. For example, if we want to have a collection of strings or integers, we need a way to put them all together. This is exactly what we are going to look at with Clojure's collections.

Put Your Clojure Data in Collections

There are a number of ways to organize your data in Clojure collections. There are *lists*, *vectors*, *maps*, and *sets*. Which one you use depends on how you need to arrange and access your data. In the following sections, we will cover all the different collections, starting with simple *lists*.

Using a List Collection

Lists are collections of things. One of the things that makes lists special is that those things come in a given order. Let's take a look at how to make a list in Clojure. We promised earlier to use some storytelling to make the code examples more fun. Now that we finally get to talk about something as exciting as lists, let's take a moment to set the scene.

When Alice chased the white rabbit down the rabbit hole, she fell down and down. In fact, she fell so long that she had time to pick up and inspect jam jars on little shelves all along the hole. Our list will have some of the various things that she saw.

To create a list in Clojure, simply put a quote in front of the parens, and put your data inside of them:

```
'(1 2 "jam" :marmalade-jar)
;; -> (1 2 "jam" :marmalade-jar)
```

We can mix and match values such as strings, integers, and keywords in our collection. Clojure doesn't mind. It also doesn't mind if you use commas to separate items in your list. It will just ignore them and treat them as whitespace:

```
'(1, 2, "jam", :bee)
;; -> (1 2 "jam" :bee)
```

You will hear the word *idiomatic* quite often in relation to Clojure. This refers to the style in which Clojurists write their code. In Clojure collections, you *can* use commas, but it is *idiomatic* not to.

Commas are ignored in Clojure. Leave them behind, and use spaces to separate your elements in a collection.

What Can We Do with Lists?

How do we manipulate these lists? For example, how do we get the first element of the list? Here we are going to need some functions to help us. You can think of the list being made up of two parts: the first element of the list, and everything else. The `first` function returns the first element of the list. The `rest` function returns a list of all of the remaining elements:

```
(first '(:rabbit :pocket-watch :marmalade :door))
;; -> :rabbit

(rest '(:rabbit :pocket-watch :marmalade :door))
;; -> (:pocket-watch :marmalade :door)
```

We are of course free to nest the `first` and `rest` functions:

```
(first (rest '(:rabbit :pocket-watch :marmalade :door)))
;; -> :pocket-watch

(first (rest (rest '(:rabbit :pocket-watch :marmalade :door))))
;; -> :marmalade

(first (rest (rest (rest '(:rabbit :pocket-watch :marmalade :door)))))
;; -> :door
```

If we get a little crazy with the `rest`s and get to the end of a list, we will find `nil` waiting for us, which means of course, nothing. In our case, it also means the end of the list:

```
(first (rest (rest (rest (rest '(:rabbit :pocket-watch :marmalade :door))))))
;; -> nil
```

At first glance, this might seem like a very strange way to traverse through a list. However, the simplicity of this turns out to be very powerful in building up recursive functions, which will we delve into more in Chapter 2.

So far we have just been constructing our lists by having all the elements in them at one time. How do we go about building up a list? The is answer is simple, yet powerful. We can build up lists with just one function, called `cons`.

The `cons` function takes two arguments. The first is the element we want to add, and the second is the list that we want to add it to. So if we want to add something to an empty list, it would look like this:

```
(cons 5 '())
;; -> (5)
```

The end of list is specified with a nil, so we could do the same thing by consing an element with nil:

```
;; building the list with a nil
(cons 5 nil)
;; -> (5)
```

From here, we can start building up more:

```
(cons 4 (cons 5 nil))
;; -> (4 5)
```

And more:

```
(cons 3 (cons 4 (cons 5 nil)))
;; -> (3 4 5)
```

And even more:

```
(cons 2 (cons 3 (cons 4 (cons 5 nil))))
;; -> (2 3 4 5)
```

Now we have built up our beautiful list, but it was a bit of work. It is good to know that we have the quote/parens shortcut available to us, as well as a list function. Each of these are easy ways to make lists out of any number of things:

```
'(1 2 3 4 5)
;; -> (1 2 3 4 5)
```

```
(list 1 2 3 4 5)
;; -> (1 2 3 4 5)
```

Lists are fine when you just want to get an element off the top of the list. But what if you have a collection of things and you want to get the element that is right in the middle? In other words, what if you need index access? This is when you need a *vector*.

Using Vectors for Collecting Data by Index

Vectors are very handy and quite common in Clojure. You can spot them by their square brackets:

```
[:jar1 1 2 3 :jar2]
;; -> [:jar1 1 2 3 :jar2]
```

The first and rest operators work on vectors:

```
(first [:jar1 1 2 3 :jar2])
;; -> :jar1
```

```
(rest [:jar1 1 2 3 :jar2])
;; -> (1 2 3 :jar2)
```

Unlike lists, in vectors, you have fast index access to the elements.

There is an nth function that allows you to access the vector element at a given index:

```
(nth [:jar1 1 2 3 :jar2] 0)
;; -> :jar1

(nth [:jar1 1 2 3 :jar2] 2)
;; -> 2
```

Another useful function is last, which returns the last element in the vector:

```
;; last with a vector
(last [:rabbit :pocket-watch :marmalade])
;; -> :marmalade

;; last with a list
(last '(:rabbit :pocket-watch :marmalade))
;; -> :marmalade
```

Although you can use nth and last on lists as well as vectors, you will get better index access performance with vectors. This is because a list needs to start at the beginning to find its way to the element it wants, as shown in Figure 1-1.

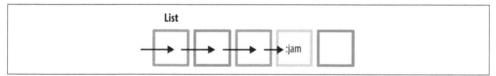

Figure 1-1. Using nth on a Clojure list

On the other hand, a vector can easily access the element, without having to traverse the whole structure to get to it, as illustrated in Figure 1-2.

Figure 1-2. Using nth on a Clojure vector

If you need to access the elements of collection by index, use a vector.

Both vectors and lists are considered Clojure *collections*. There are also other collection types that we will cover a bit later. Before we do, let's pause for a moment and talk about things that these collections have in common.

What Collections Have in Common

All collections are *immutable* and *persistent*. Immutable means that the value of the collection does not change. When we ask to cons an element to a collection, the original collection is not changed. We are returned a new version of the structure with just the element added to it. Persistent means that these collections will do *smart* creations of new versions of themselves by using structural sharing.

As we just saw in the example, collections support the sequence functions: first, rest, and last. The are a couple more collection functions we should mention as well. The count function returns the size of the collection:

```
(count [1 2 3 4])
;; -> 4
```

The conj function is rather interesting. It adds one or more elements to the collection. However, it adds them in the most natural way for that data structure. For vectors, it will add the elements at the end of the collection:

```
;; conj adds to the end of vectors
(conj [:toast :butter] :jam)
;; -> [:toast :butter :jam]

;; multiple elements added on end of vectors
(conj [:toast :butter] :jam :honey)
;; -> [:toast :butter :jam :honey]
```

Figure 1-3 illustrates using conj with a vector.

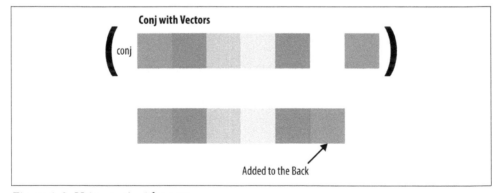

Figure 1-3. Using conj with vectors

For lists, it will add them on to the beginning:

```
;; conj adds to the front of lists
(conj '(:toast :butter) :jam)
;; -> (:jam :toast :butter)

;; multiple elements added to the front of lists
```

```
(conj '( :toast :butter) :jam :honey)
;; -> (:honey :jam :toast :butter)
```

Figure 1-4 illustrates using conj with a list.

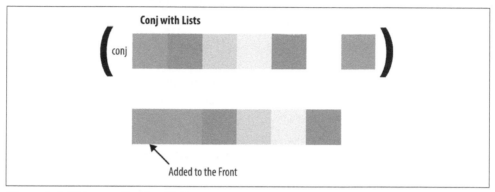

Figure 1-4. Using conj with a list

conj adds to a collection in the most natural way for the data structure. For lists, it adds to the beginning. For vectors, it adds to the end.

Ready for another type of collection? What if we want to have a collection of things that are key-value pairs? These are very useful indeed. They are called *maps* in Clojure.

Maps for Storing Key-Value Pairs of Data

Maps are extremely useful and used extensively in Clojure as a way of storing structured data by key-value pairs in an easily retrievable way. They are recognized by their curly braces:

```
{:jam1 "strawberry" :jam2 "blackberry"}
;; -> {:jam2 "blackberry", :jam1 "strawberry"}
```

Commas, again, are considered whitespace in Clojure. Maps are the one place that it can be idiomatic to leave the commas in for readability. Leave them in if it helps you:

```
{:jam1 "strawberry", :jam2 "blackberry"}
;; -> {:jam2 "blackberry", :jam1 "strawberry"}

{:jam1 "strawberry" :jam2 "blackberry"}
;; -> {:jam2 "blackberry", :jam1 "strawberry"}
```

You can get values out of maps using the get function:

```
;; explicit get
(get {:jam1 "strawberry" :jam2 "blackberry"} :jam2)
;; -> "blackberry"
```

There is also a way to provide a default if the key is not found. Simply put the default value as the last argument of the get:

```
(get {:jam1 "strawberry" :jam2 "blackberry"} :jam3 "not found")
;; -> "not found"
```

A more idiomatic way to get the value from the map without using a get, if you have a keyword as a key, is to use the key itself as a function. Keywords are by far the most common type of key used in the maps:

```
;; getting using the key as the function
(:jam2 {:jam1 "strawberry" :jam2 "blackberry" :jam3 "marmalade"})
;; -> "blackberry"
```

Which one should you use? It depends on the situation of course, but generally speaking, using the key as the function is more idiomatic. However, sometimes using an explicit get is clearer to read in the code.

The keys and vals functions return just the keys or values of the map:

```
;; the keys function
(keys {:jam1 "strawberry" :jam2 "blackberry" :jam3 "marmalade"})
;; -> (:jam3 :jam2 :jam1)

;;the vals function
(vals {:jam1 "strawberry" :jam2 "blackberry" :jam3 "marmalade"})
;; -> ("marmalade" "blackberry" "strawberry")
```

What if we need to "update" a map value? For example, if something happened to marmalade and we needed to replace it with another jam. Changing values is a pretty common thing to want to do in code. Remember, though, the collections are immutable, so when we are talking about "updating" a value, we are speaking shorthand for returning a new data structure with the updated value in it. Clojure's persistent data structures use structural sharing that does the creation very efficiently.

Remember, collections are immutable. A function to change a collection gives you back a *new* version of the collection.

The assoc function associates the new key-value pairs to map:

```
(assoc {:jam1 "red" :jam2 "black"} :jam1 "orange")
;; -> {:jam2 "black", :jam1 "orange"}
```

Given a map and a key, the dissoc function returns a new map with the key-value pair removed:

```
(dissoc {:jam1 "strawberry" :jam2 "blackberry"} :jam1)
;; -> {:jam2 "blackberry"}
```

The merge function is also quite handy to merge the key-value pairs from one map to the other:

```
(merge {:jam1 "red" :jam2 "black"}
       {:jam1 "orange" :jam3 "red"}
       {:jam4 "blue"})
;; -> {:jam4 "blue", :jam3 "red", :jam2 "black", :jam1 "orange"}
```

There is one more type of collection that we haven't covered yet. This is a collection of unique values, known as *sets*.

Using Sets for Unique Collections of Data

Sets are very useful for when you have a collection of elements with no duplicates. You can recognize them by the surrounding #{}:

```
#{:red :blue :white :pink}
;; -> #{:white :red :blue :pink}

;; No duplicates allowed in the set at creation
#{:red :blue :white :pink :pink}
;; -> IllegalArgumentException Duplicate key: :pink
```

The fact that they are sets lets us do some handy set operations as well like union, difference, and intersection. In order to use them, you will need to prefix these functions with clojure.set.

We'll see some set operations in action next. Figure 1-5 illustrates the set operations in the example.

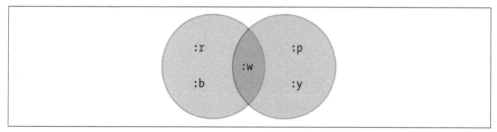

Figure 1-5. Clojure set operations

The union function takes the combined items of all of the sets:

```
(clojure.set/union #{:r :b :w} #{:w :p :y})
;; -> #{:y :r :w :b :p}
```

The difference function is almost like subtraction. It takes the elements away from one of the sets:

```
(clojure.set/difference #{:r :b :w} #{:w :p :y})
;; -> #{:r :b}
```

The intersection function returns only the shared elements between sets:

```
(clojure.set/intersection #{:r :b :w} #{:w :p :y})
;; -> #{:w}
```

You can convert another type of collection to a set using the *set* function. This is useful for using set operations on things like vectors. Maps can be converted to sets as well. The key-value pairs are turned into vectors:

```
(set [:rabbit :rabbit :watch :door])
;; -> #{:door :watch :rabbit}

(set {:a 1 :b 2 :c 3})
;; -> #{[:c 3] [:b 2] [:a 1]}
```

To get an element from a set, you can use the get function. Or if the element you are looking for is a keyword, you can access it with that, just like how a map can use the key itself as a function.

Using an example from *Alice in Wonderland*, she is looking for the rabbit in the set of all the things she can see:

```
(get #{:rabbit :door :watch} :rabbit)
;; -> :rabbit

(get #{:rabbit :door :watch} :jar)
;; -> nil
```

We can also access it directly using the keyword:

```
(:rabbit #{:rabbit :door :watch})
;; -> :rabbit
```

The set itself can be used as a function to do the same thing:

```
(#{ :rabbit :door :watch} :rabbit)
;; -> :rabbit
```

There is also a way to query the set to see if an element is there with contains?:

```
(contains? #{:rabbit :door :watch} :rabbit)
;; -> true

(contains? #{:rabbit :door :watch} :jam)
;; -> false
```

To add elements onto a set, the collection functions of conj work just fine:

```
(conj #{:rabbit :door} :jam)
;; -> #{:door :rabbit :jam}
```

The `disj` function is used to remove elements from sets:

```
(disj #{:rabbit :door} :door)
;; -> #{:rabbit}
```

Wow! Give yourself a pat on the back, we have just covered the basic structure of Clojure along with its collection data structures. Let's take a moment for a quick review.

Summary of Simple Value and Collections

You now know about simple values in Clojure:

- Strings
- Integers
- Ratios
- Decimals
- Keywords
- Characters
- Booleans

You know that these simple values can be used in functions and expressions. Expressions in Clojure include the operator or function first, followed by the parameters.

You can also use these values in collections:

- Lists are for collections of data that you want to access from the top of the list.
- Vectors are for collections of data that you want to access anywhere by position.
- Maps are for key-value pairs, which is great for organizing data and having easy access.
- Sets are for collections of unique elements; by grouping elements together in a set, you can perform set operations on them.

You also know how to use functions on these collections to build them up, get data out of them, and modify them (in an immutable way, of course).

You know about lists in Clojure, but there is something special about them. They are actually at the heart of Clojure. We will talk about why they are special next.

Lists Are the Heart of Clojure

This basic structure of Clojure comes from its LISP nature. The actual name *LISP* comes from *LISt Processing*. Lists are a key data structure.

Let's revisit a list:

```
'("marmalade-jar" "empty-jar" "pickle-jam-jar")
```

What makes this a list? The prefix quote mark on the front. Why do we need it? This is because in LISP, the first element in an expression is considered to be an operator or function. Any elements after the first are considered to be data for the operator.

This is what would happen if we didn't have it:

```
("marmalade-jar" "empty-jar" "pickle-jam-jar")
;; -> ClassCastException String cannot be cast to IFn
```

The error message is trying to tell us what we suspected—it tried to call the string as a function because it was the first element. Alas, the string—even though it is a very nice marmalade jar string—is not a function.

What would happen if we put a quote in front of the addition expression we did earlier?

```
'(+ 1 1)
;; -> (+ 1 1)
```

When the REPL evaluated it, it returned the expression rather than the number 2. Clojure considers it to now be a list of three elements:

- The first element is the operator
- The second element is the integer 1
- The third element is the integer 1

We can treat this as just a list and do things like get the first element from it:

```
(first '(+ 1 1))
;; -> +
```

All of this leads us to a very important discovery: *Code is data!*

All Clojure code is made of lists of data.

This simplicity is the heart of Clojure. It not only makes it elegant, but powerful.

We are ready for the next step. So far, we have been typing in the same code over and over again. It has been a bit repetitive. In the real world, Clojurists use *symbols* to represent data somewhat like other languages use variables. We are going to make our lives much easier by learning how to use them.

Symbols and the Art of Binding

Clojure symbols refer to values. When a symbol is evaluated, it returns the thing it refers to. So instead of typing in a specific vector of:

```
[1 2 3 4]
```

over and over again, we can assign it any symbol we like, like foo. Then when we evaluate foo, it will return the value of:

```
[1 2 3 4]
```

It is easier to see examples of symbols in action, so let's take a look at creating them with def.

def allows us to give something a name, so we can refer to it from anywhere in our code. It doesn't bind a symbol with the thing directly, it does it through a var (the reason is not important right now). Vars are not the same as variables from most other programming languages because we don't expect their values to change during the course of the program. In Clojure, there are powerful tools to handle the stuff that changes with time that we will discuss more in Chapter 3.

Let's give the string "Alice" a name:

```
(def developer "Alice")
;; -> #'user/developer
```

What did def do? It created a var object in the default namespace of our REPL called user (we will talk more about namespaces shortly), for the symbol developer. Now when we evaluate developer in the REPL, it will evaluate to "Alice". We could also reference the symbol by its namespace, which is prefixed by a slash (/). We don't have to do that in this case, because the REPL starts in the user namespace:

```
developer
;; -> "Alice"

user/developer
;; -> "Alice"
```

Vars with namespaces might seem to be quite different from the programming language you are used to. Just like you have a full name that consists of a first and a last name, which helps differentiate yourself from other people with the same first name, so vars use namespaces. The *fully qualified* name of the var includes the namespace followed by a forward slash, then the name of the var:

```
user/developer
```

In the line user/developer, user is the namespace and developer is the name of the var. We can use the shorthand version of just developer if we are in the same namespace of the var. But we can also always use the fully qualified name of the var that includes the namespace.

This is quite an exciting discovery. We now have the ability to create shorthand symbols for things and refer to them later. We no longer need to type them out all the time.

But there are a couple of problems. First, we don't really want to create a global var for all the things. Second, what do we do if we want to have a *temporary* var? An example of this is if we want to set the developer's name to a var for a specific calcuation, but we don't want to interfere with the original value.

The answer is to use let.

Using let allows us to have bindings to symbols that are only available within the context of the let. This is incredibly useful and a fundamental building block of the language. Let's looks at what happens if we change the binding of the symbol developer to "Alice in Wonderland" in a let:

```
(def developer "Alice")
;; -> #'user/developer

(let [developer "Alice in Wonderland"]
  developer)
;; -> "Alice in Wonderland"

developer
;; -> "Alice"
```

The bindings of let are in a vector form. It expects pairs of symbol and values. This is yet another example of the power of *code as data*. In fact, most everything we are learning is built on the simple structure of Clojure.

Remember, what happens in a let, stays in the let. So if you bind a symbol inside the let that doesn't exist outside, and then try to reference it later, it will give you an error:

```
(let [developer "Alice in Wonderland"
      rabbit "White Rabbit"]
  [developer rabbit])
;; -> ["Alice in Wonderland" "White Rabbit"]

rabbit
;; -> CompilerException java.lang.RuntimeException:
;; -> Unable to resolve symbol: rabbit in this context
```

Remember, what happens in a let, stays in the let.

Great! With symbols and binding we can now:

- Use def to create global vars
- Use let to create temporary bindings

We made our own data, now let's make our own functions. And because code is data, the process is very similar.

Creating Our Own Functions

Creating functions is one of the most common and important building blocks of Clojure programs. We can create functions and assign symbols to them and call them later. Clojure is a functional language, so functions are one of the main features. So far, we have just been using built-in functions to the language. But we can make our own!

Let's first look to see how to make our function with defn.

defn is very similar to def, but it creates vars for functions. It takes the following as arguments: the name of the function, a vector of parameters, and finally the body of the function. To call the function, simply use the function with parens. When we *call* a function, Clojure will evaluate it and return a result.

A function can be defined with no parameters by using an empty vector. This one takes no params and returns the string "Off we go!":

```
(defn follow-the-rabbit [] "Off we go!")
;; -> #'user/follow-the-rabbit

(follow-the-rabbit)
;; -> "Off we go!"
```

A function can also be defined with parameters. This function takes two jams and evaluates to a map containing those jams:

```
(defn shop-for-jams [jam1 jam2]
  {:name "jam-basket"
   :jam1 jam1
   :jam2 jam2})
;; -> #'user/shop-for-jams

(shop-for-jams "strawberry" "marmalade")
;; -> {:name "jam-basket", :jam1 "strawberry", :jam2 "marmalade"}
```

Sometimes you need to use a function briefly, but don't want to name it. These are *anonymous functions*. An anonymous function in Clojure can be expressed with the fn operator. It takes a vector of parameters and then the body of the function. It can be called, again, simply by calling the function with surrounding parens:

```
;;returns back a function
(fn [] (str "Off we go" "!"))
;; -> #<user$eval790$fn__791 user$eval790$fn__791@2ecd16a2>

;;invoke with parens
((fn [] (str "Off we go" "!")))
;; -> "Off we go!"
```

In fact, defn is just the same as using def and binding the name to the anonymous function:

```
(def follow-again (fn [] (str "Off we go" "!")))
;; -> #'user/follow-again

(follow-again)
;; -> "Off we go!"
```

There is a shorthand form of an anonymous function, too. It uses a # in front of the parens:

```
(#(str "Off we go" "!"))
;; -> "Off we go!"
```

If there is one parameter, you can use the percent sign (%) to represent it:

```
(#(str "Off we go" "!" " - " %) "again")
;; -> "Off we go! - again"
```

Or if there are multiple parameters, you can number the percent signs—for example, **%1**, **%2**, and so on:

```
(#(str "Off we go" "!" " - " %1 %2) "again" "?")
;; -> "Off we go! - again?"
```

You can now create all sorts of symbols. How do we keep everything organized? With object-oriented languages, we rely on objects to contain and group similar functions. Clojure does this in another way. It uses *namespaces*.

Keep Your Symbols Organized in Namespaces

Namespaces are organized and controlled access to vars. We saw that when we created a var with def or defn, it created it in the default namespace for the REPL, which is called "user." You can create your own namespace and switch to it using ns. Any vars created will now be created with this namespace.

Let's create a new namespace now. This one is going to be for Alice's favorite foods. We are going to call it `alice.favfoods`:

```
(ns alice.favfoods)
;; -> nil
```

At this point, the current namespace of the REPL has been switched from our default one that starts up the REPL to our newly defined one, `alice.favfoods`. We can check in Clojure by seeing the value that *ns* returns. The asterisks on either side of the ns are called *earmuffs* and are used as a convention for things that are intended for rebinding (to change):

```
*ns*
;; -> #<Namespace alice.favfoods>
```

If we define something here, the var will be directly accessible:

```
(def fav-food "strawberry jam")
;; -> #'alice.favfoods/fav-food

fav-food
;; -> "strawberry jam"
```

It also can be accessed via the fully qualified namespace `alice.favfoods/fav-food`:

```
alice.favfoods/fav-food
;; -> "strawberry jam"
```

If we switch to to another namespace, the symbol will no longer be resolved:

```
(ns rabbit.favfoods)
;; -> nil

fav-food
;; -> CompilerException java.lang.RuntimeException:
;; -> Unable to resolve symbol: fav-food in this context
```

We could define a var with the symbol, with a different namespace, to another value:

```
(ns rabbit.favfoods)

(def fav-food "lettuce soup")
;; -> #'rabbit.favfoods/fav-food

fav-food
;; -> "lettuce soup"
```

To refer to Alice's favorite food, we would need to evaluate the fully qualified namespace:

```
alice.favfoods/fav-food
;; -> "strawberry jam"
```

Clojure *libs* are made up of these names and symbols associated with these namespaces. There are three main ways of using libs in your namespace using `require`. The first way is to use the `require` expression with the namespace as the argument. This will simply load the lib and enable access to it via the fully qualified namespace. When we used the set functions earlier, we had to use the fully qualified namespace. Remember `clojure.set/union`?

```
;; Union
(clojure.set/union #{:r :b :w} #{:w :p :y})
;; -> #{:y :r :w :b :p}
```

The `clojure.set` namespace gets auto-required into our `user` namespace when the REPL starts up. If it didn't get loaded for us, we could do it using `require`:

```
(require 'clojure.set)
```

The second way is to use the `require` expression with an alias using `:as`. This allows access to the symbols using the alias as a prefix to the name, rather than the original namespace:

```
(ns wonderland)
;; -> nil

;; using an alias
(require '[alice.favfoods :as af])
;; -> nil

af/fav-food
;; -> "strawberry jam"
```

Although you can use `require` on its own, it is common to see it nested within the ns, with a keyword and vector:

```
(ns wonderland
  (:require [alice.favfoods :as af]))

af/fav-food
;; -> "strawberry jam"
```

The last way is to use `require` with the namespace and the `:refer` `:all` options. This loads all the symbols and makes them directly accessible in the current namespace, just by the symbol name. This can be a bit risky, because naming conflicts can occur. It is also harder to read the code and figure out which lib a function is coming from. What happens if we try to refer to the symbol `fav-food` from two different namespaces?

```
(ns wonderland
  (:require [alice.favfoods :refer :all]
            [rabbit.favfoods :refer :all]))
;; -> Exception:
;;    fav-food already refers to: #'alice.favfoods/fav-food
;;    in namespace: wonderland
```

Most Clojure code will use libs with a `require` and specify an alias using `:as`. Exceptions are tests, where it is common to use the `clojure.test` functions directly as well as the namespace you are testing. There is also a `use` expression that is the same as the `require` with `:refer` `:all`. Although the `use` is still acceptable, the `require` with `:refer` `:all` is preferred.

Let's take a moment to look at all the things you can now do!

- You can create and manipulate collections of data.
- You can create functions.
- You can create symbols.
- You can organize your code into namespaces.

Here is a nice example for practice. It is a function that takes in the rabbit's favorite foods and Alice's favorite foods and returns things that they both like to eat. It also uses our namespaces and symbols:

```
(ns wonderland
  (:require [clojure.set :as s]))   ❶

(defn common-fav-foods [foods1 foods2]
  (let [food-set1 (set foods1)       ❷
        food-set2 (set foods2)       ❸
        common-foods (s/intersection food-set1 food-set2)]   ❹
    (str "Common Foods: " common-foods)))

(common-fav-foods [:jam :brownies :toast]
                  [:lettuce :carrots :jam])
;; -> "Common Foods: #{:jam}"
```

❶ We require the `clojure.set` namespace and we are going to use the shorthand letter s to refer to it.

❷   The set of `foods1` is bound to a symbol `food-set1`

❸   The set of `foods2` is bound to a symbol `food-set2`

❹   We use the intersection function from the `clojure.set` namespace and use the symbols `food-set1` and `food-set2`.

You are on your way in your journey to Clojure understanding. You have the ability to structure your Clojure code into simple and beautiful expressions. You know how to fill these expressions with simple values like integers and strings, or Clojure collections, like maps and vectors. You can create global symbolic bindings with `def` and `defn`, and local bindings in a `let`. You can even organize these bindings into namespaces. Finally, you know of the true nature of Clojure's code as data. With all these fundamentals under your belt, you are ready to move on to the next chapter where we will take this structure of code and make it move and flow with functional transformations.

CHAPTER 2

Flow and Functional Transformations

We saw the structure of Clojure in Chapter 1. You now can create collections and manipulate them. In this chapter, we are going to see how to make our code come to life. First, we will learn how to control the logic flow, starting with logic tests, then moving on to some basic control flow forms. While we are at it, we will also cover some useful functions that create other functions. Next, we will take a look at *destructuring*. Destructuring is a process that can pull apart and give names to collection elements that you care about, making them more readable.

After that, we will take a look at the lazy nature of Clojure. In doing so, we will explore the power of lazy evaluation and how it will let us deal with infinite lists. All this will get us ready to explore a very import concept, which is *recursion*. With recursion, we will look at how the structure of Clojure and functional programming fit together to transform code beautifully. Finally, we will take a look at some fundamental forms in Clojure that are key to shaping data in a functional way.

This chapter is a lot to take in, so don't get discouraged if it doesn't click into place at once. Let the examples wash right now. They will soak into a good understanding when we put it all to practice in Part II.

One more thing before we dive in. Let's talk about some terminology. Sometimes we talk about *expressions* and sometimes we talk about *forms*. What exactly do they mean? Are they the same thing? They do, indeed, mean different things. In fact, it may be no surprise that people can argue on the exact meaning. But for the purposes of this book, an expression is code that can be evaluated for a result, and a form is a *valid* expression that can be evaluated. It differs from an expression in that it specifies a correct syntax by being valid. Let's look at some examples.

This is an expression:

```
(first [1 2 4])
;; -> 1
```

This is a form because its syntax is correct and it runs without errors:

```
(first [:a :b :c])
;; -> :a
```

However, the following is not a valid form because it has syntax errors. The `first` function does not work without an argument:

```
(first)
;; -> ArityException
```

The term *expression* tends to be more common in everyday use. All in all, these distinctions are nice to know, but don't get hung up on the specific term if we use one rather than the other. In all cases, we mean the code that we run to evaluate for a result.

With that last item under our belts, let's take a look at what we need to control the flow of data in our code.

Controlling the Flow with Logic

To control the flow of data, we need logic operations. We already saw that Clojure has the boolean data types:

- `true`
- `false`

In fact, if we look at the class of these values with the *class* function in Clojure, we can see that they are just plain `java.lang.Booleans` from Java:

```
(class true)
;; -> java.lang.Boolean
```

Let's try some of this truthy stuff out.

How can you tell if something is true? There is a function to answer that very question. Not surprisingly, it is called `true?`. It is a convention with Clojure functions that if the result returns a boolean, it is named with a question mark at the end.

Let's run `true?` through some exercises:

```
(true? true)
;; -> true

(true? false)
;; -> false
```

How can you tell if something is false? You most likely guessed that there is also a
`false?` function:

```
(false? false)
;; -> true

(false? true)
;; -> false
```

What about other things we can test for? For example, how do we test if something is
not there? In Clojure, `nil` represents the absence of a value. We can test for it by
using `nil?`:

```
(nil? nil)
;; -> true

(nil? 1)
;; -> false
```

No surprises there. What about negation? How do we check if something is not true?
There is a `not` that will do that for us. The `not` returns true if the parameter is a logical false; otherwise, it returns false:

```
(not true)
;; -> false

(not false)
;; -> true
```

Here is where it gets interesting. `nil` is treated as logically false in some logical tests.
So the opposite of that would be true:

```
(not nil)
;; -> true
```

If you are coming from a language like Java, that might surprise you at first. If it did,
say to yourself "`nil` is logically false" three times.

 Remember, `nil` is logically false in tests.

Likewise, a `not` of some other value than a logical false, like a string or an integer, will
return false:

```
(not "hi")
;; -> false
```

This might get you wondering about how to do comparisons. We will cover how to check whether or not values are equal next.

How do we tell if something is equal to something else? We can use an equals sign (=). It returns true if the two parameters are equal to each other. For those of you with a Java background, this equality is the same as Java's `equals` method.

Let's bring *Alice in Wonderland* back into our code examples. What is Alice doing now? Last time we checked, she fell down the rabbit hole. Now she is wondering whether or not to drink a bottle labeled "drinkme."

Let's check equality of the two labels of these bottles:

```
(= :drinkme :drinkme)
;; -> true
```

Of course, it will be false if they don't match:

```
(= :drinkme 4)
;; -> false
```

Collection equality is special:

```
(= '(:drinkme :bottle) [:drinkme :bottle])
;; -> true
```

There also is a `not=` expression that is a shortcut for doing `(not (= x y))`:

```
(not= :drinkme :4)
;; -> true
```

You now know how to perform basic logic tests. Let's take a moment to review before moving on:

- `true?` tests for true values
- `false?` tests for false values
- `nil` is treated the same as logical `false`
- `nil` is treated the same as logical `false` (repeated on purpose—`false` and `nil` are the only logically false values)
- `nil?` tests for the absence of a value
- `not` tests for the negation of the value
- `=` tests for equality
- `not=` tests for inequality

You are well prepared to go onto to other sorts of logical tests that we need to consider.

Let's take a look at how to perform some tests on collection in Clojure. For example, how do you tell if a vector is empty? There are some tests that are specifically for collections, and we will look at a few rather useful ones. We will also talk about some important abstractions that Clojure uses.

Logic Tests You Can Use on Collections

Let's start out by considering how to answer the question of how to tell if a vector is empty. Thankfully, we don't need to consider it too long, because there is an `empty?` function. You can check to see if a vector, list, or map is empty by using `empty?`.

Let's take an example of the things that Alice saw when she landed, finally, at the bottom of the rabbit hole:

```
(empty? [:table :door :key])
;; -> false

(empty? [])
;; -> true

(empty? {})
;; -> true

(empty? '())
;; -> true
```

If we look at the actual definition of `empty?` we can see that it is the same thing as using a `not_ _seq` on the collection:

```
(defn empty?
    [coll] (not (seq coll)))
```

What is `seq`? To understand that, let's step back and talk about abstractions. In Clojure, there are the *collection* and *sequence* abstractions. The collections are simply a collection of elements, like vectors, lists, and maps. They share the persistent, immutable data structure by implementing the clojure.lang.IPersistentCollection interface. The collections support shared methods such as `count`, `conj`, and `seq`. The seq function turns the collection into a *sequence*. A sequence is a walkable list abstraction for the collection data structure. `seq` (short for sequences), are also persistent and immutable and provide the shared functions `first`, `rest`, and `cons`. The `seq` function returns a `seq` on the collection or `nil` if it is empty:

```
(seq [1 2 3])
;; -> (1 2 3)

(class [1 2 3])
;; -> clojure.lang.PersistentVector

(class (seq [1 2 3]))
```

```
;; -> clojure.lang.PersistentVector$ChunkedSeq

(seq [])
;; -> nil
```

A number of expressions in Clojure deal with collections that make use of `seq` under the covers to make life easier for you. An example of this is how the `first` function works when we call it on a vector. Normally, if it is a collection, we should have to convert it to a `seq` before going any further. However, we don't have to call `seq` on the collection, because the `first` actually calls `seq` on its argument in the implementation for us. So reviewing the `empty?` function, we can use it to check if a collection is empty. If you want to check if a collection is not empty, on the other hand, it is idiomatic to use the `seq` function rather than `(not (empty? x))`:

```
(empty? [])
;; -> true

;; use this to check for not empty
(seq [])
;; -> nil
```

Remember, use `seq` to check for not empty instead of `(not (empty? x))`. This is because `nil` is treated as logically false in tests, whereas a non-nil value like [1 3 4] is treated as logically true.

Returning back to look at more collections tests, how do you test if something is true for every element in the collection? The `every?` function can do this. It takes a predicate to test and the collection as the arguments. If the predicate evaluates to true for every item in the collection, it will return true; otherwise, it returns false:

```
(every? odd? [1 3 5])
;; -> true

(every? odd? [1 2 3 4 5])
;; -> false
```

Wait. What is a predicate? A predicate is just a function that returns a value used in a logic test.

The predicate in collection tests takes an element from the collection as its argument. We can define our own function to use as the predicate. What about a function that would test if the bottle labeled "drinkme" is drinkable? In naming the function, it is good to note that we are using a question mark on the end. It is idiomatic in Clojure to use a question mark in the name if it returns a boolean:

```
(defn drinkable? [x]
  (= x :drinkme))
;; -> #'user/drinkable?

(every? drinkable? [:drinkme :drinkme])
;; -> true

(every? drinkable? [:drinkme :poison])
;; -> false
```

We could also have used an anonymous function instead:

```
(every? (fn [x] (= x :drinkme)) [:drinkme :drinkme])
;; -> true
```

In Chapter 1, we learned that there is a shorthand version of the anonymous function that we could use instead:

```
(every? #(= % :drinkme) [:drinkme :drinkme])
;; -> true
```

We just saw a way to test for something to be true for every element in a collection. What about the opposite? How do we tell if it is true of "not any" of the elements?

The `not-any?` function takes a predicate for a collection and returns false if it is true for any element in the collection:

```
(not-any? #(= % :drinkme) [:drinkme :poison])
;; -> false

(not-any? #(= % :drinkme) [:poison :poison])
;; -> true
```

We have seen `every?` and `not-any?`, but there is another important case to consider. What if we want to test to see if "some" of the elements in the collection pass our logic test?

`some` takes a predicate as well for a collection, but it does something a little bit different. It returns the first logical true value of the predicate, `nil` otherwise. In the following example, it will return true if one of the elements is greater than 3:

```
(some #(> % 3) [1 2 3 4 5])
;; -> true
```

This is very useful for testing whether or not an element is in a sequence by using a set as a predicate. It is important to remember that a non-`nil` value of the predicate is also considered a logical true. Also, note that a set is a function of its member:

```
(#{1 2 3 4 5} 3)
;; -> 3
```

So, the some function can be used with a set to return the element, or the first matching element of the sequence:

```
(some #{3} [1 2 3 4 5])
;; -> 3

(some #{4 5} [1 2 3 4 5])
;; -> 4
```

But be careful with logically false values:

```
(some #{nil} [nil nil nil])
;; -> nil

(some #{false} [false false false])
;; -> nil
```

Phew! In addition to all the base logic tests, now you know how to do logic tests on collections too.

You can now:

- Test to see if a collection is empty with empty?
- Test to see if a collection is not empty with seq
- Test to see if all the elements test true with every?
- Test to see if all of the elements test false with not-any?
- Test to see if some of the elements test true with some

Harnessing the Power of Flow Control

Now that we have covered some ways of doing logical tests, we are finally ready to look at some control structures. We will cover some common ones, if and when, along with their corresponding helpful if-let and when-let expressions. Then, we move on to the flexible cond and case. First up is the important if.

if takes three parameters. The first parameter is the expression that is the logical test. If the test expression evaluates to true, the second parameter is evaluated. If not, the last parameter is evaluated:

```
(if true "it is true" "it is false")
;; -> "it is true"

(if false "it is true" "it is false")
;; -> "it is false"

(if nil "it is true" "it is false")
;; -> "it is false"
```

```
(if (= :drinkme :drinkme)
  "Try it"
  "Don't try it")
;; -> "Try it"
```

There is a nice expression to combine a let with the if. This is for the case where you want to test something, but you also want to remember it.

The if-let allows you to bind an expression to a symbol, and if it is logical true, it then evaluates the first argument, otherwise the last argument. This can be a more compact way of doing a let and then an if. This is quite useful when binding expressions that are only used conditionally:

```
(let [need-to-grow-small (> 5 3)]
  (if need-to-grow-small
    "drink bottle"
    "don't drink bottle"))
;; -> "drink bottle"

;; This example is a bit contrived, because we could just do a
;; regular if, but it is good for illustration purposes.
(if-let [need-to-grow-small (> 5 1)]
  "drink bottle"
  "don't drink bottle")
;; -> "drink bottle"
```

An if is what you want, when you have two possible things you want to do depending on the result of your logic test. In particular, you want to do one thing when it is true, and another thing when it is false. What if you don't really care about doing two things? If you only want to do one thing when your test is true, and don't really care to do anything when it is false, you can use a when.

The when takes a predicate, and if it is logical true, it will evaluate the body. Otherwise, it returns nil. This is useful when you only want to evaluate an expression if some sort of key or flag is present. Let's make a function that could have Alice drink the bottle when she needed to grow small:

```
(defn drink [need-to-grow-small]
  (when need-to-grow-small "drink bottle"))

(drink true)
;; -> "drink bottle"

(drink false)
;; -> nil
```

There is a similar expression to if-let for a when, and it is called when-let.

The same sort of thing is true for the when-let. It binds the logical test to a symbol and evaluates the expression if it is logical true, otherwise returns nil. In this example, it is binding the `true` value to `need-to-grow-small`. Because it is true, it will return the "drink bottle" value:

```
(when-let [need-to-grow-small true]
  "drink bottle")
;; -> "drink bottle"
```

In this example, `need-to-grow-small` is bound to the `false` value. It won't then return the "drink bottle" value; instead, it will return `nil`:

```
(when-let [need-to-grow-small false]
  "drink bottle")
;; -> nil
```

We can now control our flow of code with `if`s and `when`s. But what if we want to test for multiple things? We could nest `if`s, but that gets ugly very quickly. It's better to use a `cond` to take multiple expressions.

The `cond` expression takes pairs of expressions to test and an expression to then evaluate if the test expression returns a logical true. This might be similar to `if` and `elsif` expressions in other languages you are used to:

```
(let [bottle "drinkme"]
  (cond
    (= bottle "poison") "don't touch"
    (= bottle "drinkme") "grow smaller"
    (= bottle "empty") "all gone"))
;; -> "grow smaller"
```

In the `cond` clauses, once a logical test returns true and the expression is evaluated, none of the other test clauses are tried. So, the order of the tests are important:

```
(let [x 5]
  (cond
    (> x 10) "bigger than 10"
    (> x 4) "bigger than 4"
    (> x 3) "bigger than 3"))
;; -> "bigger than 4"
```

Again, order is important. Look what happens if we move the "bigger than 3" clause to the top. The first match stops the evaluation and returns:

```
(let [x 5]
  (cond
    (> x 3) "bigger than 3"
    (> x 10) "bigger than 10"
    (> x 4) "bigger than 4"))
;; -> "bigger than 3"
```

If none of the tests match, a `nil` is returned:

```
(let [x 1]
  (cond
```

```
    (> x 10) "bigger than 10"
    (> x 4) "bigger than 4"
    (> x 3) "bigger than 3"))
;; -> nil
```

We can add a default clause by simply adding the keyword :else as the last test expression. We can also use cond with a default clause to replace the if/elsif/else formulation that you find in other languages:

```
(let [bottle "mystery"]
  (cond
    (= bottle "poison") "don't touch"
    (= bottle "drinkme") "grow smaller"
    (= bottle "empty") "all gone"
    :else "unknown"))
;; -> "unknown"
```

There is nothing special about using the :else keyword. It is simply the fact that it is a keyword that evaluates as a logical true. We could just as well use anything else that would do the job, like a string called "default":

```
(let [bottle "mystery"]
  (cond
    (= bottle "poison") "don't touch"
    (= bottle "drinkme") "grow smaller"
    (= bottle "empty") "all gone"
    "default" "unknown"))
;; -> "unknown"
```

If the test expression in your cond is just testing one value (like in the previous example), there is a more concise expression to use.

The case is a shortcut for the cond where there is only one test value and it can be compared with an =:

```
(let [bottle "drinkme"]
  (case bottle
    "poison" "don't touch"
    "drinkme" "grow smaller"
    "empty" "all gone"))
```

If no match is found, however, the behavior of the case is much different than the cond. Instead of returning nil for no matching test expression, the case statement will return an error that there is no matching clause:

```
(let [bottle "mystery"]
  (case bottle
    "poison" "don't touch"
    "drinkme" "grow smaller"
    "empty" "all gone"))
;; -> IllegalArgumentException No matching clause: mystery
```

A default for the `case` is one optional, last expression that is evaluated if there are no matching clauses found:

```
(let [bottle "mystery"]
  (case bottle
    "poison" "don't touch"
    "drinkme" "grow smaller"
    "empty" "all gone"
    "unknown"))
  ;; -> "unknown"
```

You now have full control of your code with test expressions and flow control expressions. You can:

- Use `if` for branch control
- Use `when` for evaluating expressions when a test is true
- Use `cond` for testing multiple expressions
- Use `case` for a nice shortcut for single-value `cond` tests

Before we move on, let's take a moment to cover some useful expressions that create other functions. This comes in handy when you want to combine two functions together to make one new function, or perhaps partially apply a function and create a new function for it and use it later. We have seen how to create functions with `defn`, `fn`, and the `#` `()` shortcut. Now, you will have some additional functions in your toolbox.

Functions Creating Functions and Other Neat Expressions

Let's say you have a function that takes two arguments, but you only know the value of one of the arguments. You also would really like to apply that function now—just partially, not all the way. You will finish it up when you get the other parameter. You can do that with `partial`.

`partial` is a way of currying in Clojure. The technique of currying is the process of taking a function that takes multiple arguments and transforming it into a chain of single argument functions.

Currying is not a cooking term for preparing a tasty dish, but a way to generate a new function with an argument partially applied.

Let's illustrate this with an example using Alice. We have a `grow` function that takes two parameters: one is the name of the person growing and the second is how she should grow (big or small). It will use str, which takes arguments and returns the concatenated string of them to construct a sentence of how the person is growing:

```
(defn grow [name direction]
  (if (= direction :small)
    (str name " is growing smaller")
    (str name " is growing bigger")))
;; -> #'user/grow

(grow "Alice" :small)
;; -> "Alice is growing smaller"

(grow "Alice" :big)
;; -> "Alice is growing bigger"
```

We can take this original grow function of two parameters and change it into a function with one parameter of just the direction, with the name "Alice" already ready to be applied:

```
(partial grow "Alice")
;; -> #<core$partial$fn__4228 clojure.core$partial$fn__4228@1759817d>

((partial grow "Alice") :small)
;; -> "Alice is growing smaller"
```

Using partial is a powerful technique, but sometimes you need something different. If you want to combine multiple functions into one function, you can use comp.

comp creates a new function that combines other functions. It takes any number of functions as its parameters and returns the composition of those functions going from right to left. Let's look at this in an example, where we want a function that would toggle the direction of growing big or small:

```
(defn toggle-grow [direction]
  (if (= direction :small) :big :small))
;; -> #'user/toggle-grow

(toggle-grow :big)
;; -> :small

(toggle-grow :small)
;; -> :big
```

Then we wanted Alice to have a function that would generate a string about what direction she was growing:

```
(defn oh-my [direction]
  (str "Oh My! You are growing " direction))
;; -> #'user/oh-my
```

To have Alice grow big after being small and then say "oh my," we could simply call one function and then the other:

```
(oh-my (toggle-grow :small))
;; -> "Oh My! You are growing :big"
```

Or, we could use `comp` to create a function that was the composition of the two:

```
(defn surprise [direction]
  ((comp oh-my toggle-grow) direction))

(surprise :small)
;; -> "Oh My! You are growing :big"
```

Both `partial` and `comp` are very useful ways to create elegant, concise code. You now have some useful functions that make other functions in your toolbox.

Now is a good time to take a break and let this wash over you. Here is an example with `partial` if you want to practice some more (otherwise, take a breath and forge on):

```
(defn adder [x y]
  (+ x y))
;; -> #'user/adder

(adder 3 4)
;; -> 7

(def adder-5 (partial adder 5))
;; -> #'user/adder-5

(adder-5 10)
;; -> 15
```

Speaking of breaks, that is the next way that we are going to transform our code. We are going to be breaking it up into bindings that make it more understandable. It is a technique called *destructuring*.

Destructuring

Destructuring allows you to assign named bindings for the elements in things like vectors and maps. Let's take a look at an example of destructuring using `let` and a vector of doors that Alice saw leading to the garden:

```
(let [[color size] ["blue" "small"]]
  (str "The " color " door is " size))
;; -> "The blue door is small"
```

What just happened here? Let's look at the vector in the `let` with our string values in it:

```
["blue" "small"]
```

The values were assigned to two named bindings, `color` and `size`. The destructuring knew what values to bind by the placement of the symbols in the binding expression.

In this case, it knew to look at the first element in the vector and bind it to the symbol color. Then the next element in the vector would be bound to the symbol size:

```
[[color size]]
```

We also could have written this same thing in a let without destructuring:

```
(let [x ["blue" "small"]
      color (first x)
      size (last x)]
  (str "The " color " door is " size))
;; -> "The blue door is small"
```

This code without destructuring is more verbose. If we want to break down a data structure in a sequential fashion, we can use the vector destructuring to achieve more concise, readable, and elegant code. It also handles nesting quite easily:

```
(let [[color [size]] ["blue" ["very small"]]]
  (str "The " color " door is " size))
;; -> "The blue door is very small"
```

What if we want to keep the whole initial data structure as a binding, as well as breaking down the expression into individual bindings with destructuring? There is an :as keyword that lets us do just that:

```
(let [[color [size] :as original] ["blue" ["small"]]]
  {:color color :size size :original original})
;; -> {:color "blue", :size "small", :original ["blue" ["small"]]}
```

Destructuring can also be done with maps. In the let we can assign binding to the value of the keys in the map. We can show an example of this with the flowers Alice saw in the garden:

```
(let [{flower1 :flower1 flower2 :flower2}
      {:flower1 "red" :flower2 "blue"}]
  (str "The flowers are " flower1 " and " flower2))
;; -> "The flowers are red and blue"
```

We can even specify default values to use for the keys if they are not found in the map with :or:

```
(let [{flower1 :flower1 flower2 :flower2 :or {flower2 "missing"}}
      {:flower1 "red"}]
  (str "The flowers are " flower1 " and " flower2))
;; -> "The flowers are red and missing"
```

To keep the whole initial data structure as a binding, :as works in maps too:

```
(let [{flower1 :flower1 :as all-flowers}
      {:flower1 "red"}]
  [flower1 all-flowers])
;; -> ["red" {:flower1 "red"}]
```

Because most of the time, you will want to give the same name to the binding as the name of the key, there is a nice shortcut using the :keys directive. This takes a vector of the keys and values that you want to get out of the incoming map. You will see this a lot in Clojure code, because it is one of the most commonly used ways of destructuring:

```
(let [{:keys [flower1 flower2]}
      {:flower1 "red" :flower2 "blue"}]
  (str "The flowers are " flower1 " and " flower2))
;; -> "The flowers are red and blue"
```

This destructuring is also available to use on parameters while defining functions with defn. This is a useful way to not only bind the incoming parameters in their structure, but also to document what the incoming structure looks like. If we have the following function for constructing the string about flower colors from the map:

```
(defn flower-colors [colors]
  (str "The flowers are "
       (:flower1 colors)
       " and "
       (:flower2 colors)))

(flower-colors {:flower1 "red" :flower2 "blue"})
;; -> "The flowers are red and blue"
```

We can certainly read the body of the code and understand that the colors parameter is a map with the keys :flower1 and :flower2 in it. But if we put the destructuring in the parameters in, it makes it even clearer, just by looking at the function signature. It also makes the code more concise by not needing a let for the bindings:

```
(defn flower-colors [{:keys [flower1 flower2]}]
  (str "The flowers are " flower1 " and " flower2))

(flower-colors {:flower1 "red" :flower2 "blue"})
;; -> "The flowers are red and blue"
```

You now know how to transform your code into more understandable pieces with destructuring. We are next going to look at a way to harness the power of laziness and make it work to your advantage.

The laziness we are talking about is not unlike the force of inertia that is felt in a really comfy chair. It is the power not to evaluate all the things. You might not think that this is an advantage until your are up against something as daunting as infinite lists. This is when Clojure shines and unleashes its special power. The power of laziness!

The Power of Laziness

In addition to regular collections and lists, Clojure can also work with infinite lists! It is hard to believe, but it is true. Let's try it by taking the first five numbers from all the positive integers:

```
(take 5 (range))
;; -> (0 1 2 3 4)

(take 10 (range))
;; -> (0 1 2 3 4 5 6 7 8 9)
```

It does this with something called *lazy sequences*. Calling `range` returns a lazy sequence. You can specify an end for the range by passing it a parameter:

```
(range 5)
;; -> (0 1 2 3 4)

(class (range 5))
;; -> clojure.lang.LazySeq
```

But when you don't specify an end, the default is infinity. You need to take special care with infinite sequences. For example, if you were to evaluate this expression in your REPL, it would make it crash:

```
;;DON"T EVALUATE THIS OR YOUR REPL WILL CRASH
(range)
```

Why is that a bad idea? Because, when we ask our REPL to evaluate the infinite sequence, we are destroying the lazy part by asking it to give us the result. It will try to put *all* of infinity, which is really a bit too much for even our powerful REPL to handle.

 Don't evaluate an infinite sequence directly in your REPL. It will cause it to try to evaluate and realize the whole sequence ... and infinity is really a lot.

What does the `take` do that allows us to interact safely with these lazy sequences? Instead of trying to realize and evaluate the results for the entire infinite sequence, it only evaluates the number of items that we asked it to:

```
(take 10 (range))
;; -> (0 1 2 3 4 5 6 7 8 9)
```

Even if we ask it to take 1,000 or 100,000, it will still be considerably less than infinity:

```
(count (take 1000 (range)))
;; -> 1000
```

```
(count (take 100000 (range)))
;; -> 100000
```

There are other ways to generate lazy sequences, and likewise, infinite sequences. repeat can be used to generate an infinite sequence of repeated items. Like range, it can take a number of times that we would like it to repeat. It also, of course, returns a lazy sequence:

```
(repeat 3 "rabbit")
;; -> ("rabbit" "rabbit" "rabbit")

(class (repeat 3 "rabbit"))
;; -> clojure.lang.LazySeq
```

Just like range, if we don't specify an end, it will be infinite:

```
(take 5 (repeat "rabbit"))
;; -> ("rabbit" "rabbit" "rabbit" "rabbit" "rabbit")

(count (take 5000 (repeat "rabbit")))
;; -> 5000
```

What if we wanted to generate an infinite sequence of randomly generated numbers? We can use rand-int to generate a random int between 0 and 10:

```
(rand-int 10)
;; -> 3

(rand-int 10)
;; -> 4
```

Could we just use this with a repeat to get a sequence of random integers? Let's test it out on just five items:

```
(repeat 5 (rand-int 10))
;; -> (7 7 7 7 7)
```

The result is not exactly random. The reason is that we should be using repeatedly instead of repeat. Where repeat returns a value over and over again, repeatedly takes a function that will be repeatedly executed over and over again. So, it will actually generate a new random integer for every element we ask for in the sequence. We only need to make a slight change. repeatedly takes a function of no arguments. Currently our (rand-int 10) returns an integer. We need to wrap it in a function. We can do this using the anonymous function shorthand that we saw earlier. When this function is called, our random integer is returned:

```
#(rand-int 10)
;; -> #<user$eval721$fn__722 user$eval721$fn__722@308092db>

(#(rand-int 10))
;; -> 3
```

Now we are ready to try again, this time with `repeatedly`:

```
(repeatedly 5 #(rand-int 10))
;; -> (1 5 8 4 3)
```

We can now generate an infinite sequence of random integers and take from it:

```
(take 10 (repeatedly #(rand-int 10)))
;; -> (9 9 5 8 3 1 0 9 3 2)
```

We will talk about one more way of generating infinite lazy sequences before moving on. This is with `cycle`. It takes a collection as an argument and returns a lazy sequence of the items in the collection repeated infinitely. Make sure you handle `cycle` with care, using a `take`, or you will crash your REPL with its infinite nature:

```
(take 3 (cycle ["big" "small"]))
;; -> ("big" "small" "big")

(take 6 (cycle ["big" "small"]))
;; -> ("big" "small" "big" "small" "big" "small")
```

So far we have only interacted with our infinite lazy sequences with `take`. But other Clojure sequence functions will work on it as well, and `rest` will return a lazy sequence when it operates on a lazy sequence:

```
(take 3 (rest (cycle ["big" "small"])))
;; -> ("small" "big" "small")
```

You just manipulated infinity. Take a moment to let it sink in.

This infinite laziness and laziness in general is important because it allows us to create code in a general and elegant way, but only use what we need in processing and memory. It is an incredibly useful tool when you are dealing with operations that take a lot of computation, or even talking to a database and chunking results as you want to process them.

Are you ready for the next frontier? We are going to tackle recursion.

Recursion

Recursion seems magical at first. Recursive functions are ones that call themselves. At first, this might seem like a very strange thing to do. But we will see how it is a very elegant way to traverse through data structures. In Clojure, and functional programming, it is the way to iterate through a sequence.

Let's take a very simple example of having a vector of adjectives that we want to traverse through and turn into a short string about Alice. She started off normal size, then she was too small, and then too big. Poor Alice, she was so upset about it she started crying while fanning herself with the rabbit's fan. The fan made her shrink and she ended up swimming and being swept away by her tears.

Our input is:

```
["normal" "too small" "too big" "swimming"]
```

We would like the output of our function to be:

```
["Alice is normal"
 "Alice is too small"
 "Alice is too big"
 "Alice is swimming"]
```

For each element in the vector, we want to transform it with the following function:

```
#(str "Alice is " %)
```

When we do this with recursion, we need to add an extra parameter to our function to keep track of the incremental building up of our desired output vector. Let's look at the function and step through it a bit at a time:

```
(def adjs ["normal"
           "too small"
           "too big"
           "is swimming"])

(defn alice-is [in out]
  (if (empty? in) ❶
    out ❷
    (alice-is ❸
     (rest in) ❹
     (conj out ❺
           (str "Alice is " (first in))))))

(alice-is adjs [])
;; -> ["Alice is normal" "Alice is too small"
;;     "Alice is too big" "Alice is swimming"]
```

What is happening here?

❶ We check to see if the input vector is empty.

❷ If so, we are done processing and we are ready to return the result.

❸ If we are not done, we start over and call the same function with different inputs.

❹ In the first position, we give it the rest of the original input.

❺ In the second position, we apply the string to the element and then append the result to the output vector.

The heart of this recursive function is using `first` and `rest` to traverse through the elements, controlling the building up of the result with `conj`, rebinding the parameters with new values on each recursive call, and finally, giving a terminating condition.

Although this is basic recursion, Clojure makes things easier by providing loop. We could rewrite the previous example using a loop:

```
(defn alice-is [input]
  (loop [in input  ❶
         out []]
    (if (empty? in)
      out
      (recur (rest in) ❷
             (conj out
                   (str "Alice is " (first in)))))))

(alice-is adjs)
;; -> ["Alice is Alice is normal"
;;     "Alice is Alice is too small"
;;     "Alice is Alice it too big"
;;     "Alice is Alice is swimming"]
```

❶ recur jumps back to the recursion point, which is the beginning of the loop, and re-binds the new parameters to the parameters.

❷ The loop used a recur instead of calling a named function.

The loop/recur construct makes our alice-is function much nicer because we can call it with only one parameter, the vector of adjectives. The loop hides the empty out vector we need for processing.

A loop is a construct that executes code several times inside the loop, called the *body*. The number of times it is executed can be until a condition is met or indefinitely.

Using recur also has another very important advantage. It provides a way of not "consuming the stack" for recursive calls. Let's construct a very simple example of this—countdown. We can naively define it as:

```
(defn countdown [n]
  (if (= n 0)
    n
    (countdown (- n 1))))

(countdown 3)
;; -> 0
```

```
(countdown 100000)
;; -> StackOverflowError
```

Why did we get a `StackOverflow`? Because in our recursive call, a new frame was added to the stack for every function call. That is a lot of frames, and a really big stack, before it even starts to evaluate things.

We could rewrite this with a `recur` and it will actually return the result:

```
(defn countdown [n]
  (if (= n 0)
    n
    (recur (- n 1))))


(countdown 100000)
;; -> 0
```

The `recur` is how Clojure avoids this stack consumption, by evaluating the function arguments and defining a position where the call is going to "jump" back to the recursion point. This way, it only needs one stack at a time. In this case, the recursion point is the function itself, because there is no loop. In general, always use `recur` when you are doing recursive calls.

We have seen how to do recursion in Clojure. This is a fundamental building block of the language, but there are also useful abstractions built upon this that you should favor over `recur`. The most commonly used expressions are the abstractions that *shape* and *transform* collections. In fact, once you master the use of these, you will begin to see how functional programming is about shaping data. It is all about *transforming* the incoming collection to a new data structure being returned. With the side effects and mutable state stripped away, the beauty of these pure transformations shines through.

The Functional Shape of Data Transformations

We will take a look at two main ways to transform collections: `map` and `reduce`. They both work on collections, but the *shape* of the results are very different. The shape of the `map` result will be the same as the incoming collection. This means that the number of elements in the resulting collection will be the same as the incoming collection. By contrast, `reduce` takes an incoming collection, but it can change the *shape* of the output data. It can change the number of elements in the collection returned. If you look at the source implementation of both `map` and `reduce`, you will see that they both use fundamental recursion to process the elements of the collection. They are higher level abstractions. Together, they are very powerful tools for transforming collections. Let's take a look at each of them.

Map the Ultimate

`map` takes a function as an argument and a collection. The function is one that will take as an argument the element of the collection. The result of `map` will be a collection with the function applied to each element. It is always easier to see what is happening with an example. Alice in her adventures fell into a pool. In the pool, there were other animals that had fallen in. We will take the vectors of animals that were swimming with her:

```
(def animals [:mouse :duck :dodo :lory :eaglet])
```

Because each of these are keywords, let's have a function that will transform a keyword to a string. `str` will do just fine for this:

```
(#(str %) :mouse)
;; -> ":mouse"
```

Finally, let's put it all together with `map` and map this function over all the elements of the collection:

```
(map #(str %) animals)
;; -> (":mouse" ":duck" ":dodo" ":lory" ":eaglet")
```

Did you notice that it wasn't a vector that got returned?

```
(class (map #(str %) animals))
;; -> clojure.lang.LazySeq
```

`map` returns a lazy sequence. Lazy sequences mean that we can deal with infinite sequences if we like. Let's see what happens when we try to map across an infinite sequence like all integers:

```
(take 3 (map #(str %) (range)))
;; -> ("0" "1" "2")

(take 10 (map #(str %) (range)))
;; -> ("0" "1" "2" "3" "4" "5" "6" "7" "8" "9")
```

With the power of lazy sequences and recursion, we can process functions easily against infinite sequences! It is OK to pause for a moment and savor how cool this really is.

Laziness needs to be handled with care. This is very important to remember when working with functions that have side effects. What is a side effect? A *pure* function is one that, given the same input, always returns the same output, without any other observable interaction with the world. An example of a pure function is adding two numbers together. A *side effect* is something else that occurs in the function that changes something in the outside world somehow. The outside world change can be something like printing to the console, logging to a file, or mutating state.

When we combine functions with side effects and laziness, we must be careful to make sure that the side effects are being executed when we want them to. In the case of map, just calling the function won't force the lazy evaluation on all the elements. We can see this by calling map with a println, which takes arguments and prints to the output stream as a side effect. Note that it returns nil:

```
(println "Look at the mouse!")
;; Look at the mouse!
;; -> nil
```

Let's see what happens if we print the animal out instead of returning a string and bind it to a var:

```
(def animal-print  (map #(println %) animals))
;; -> #'user/animal-print
```

We didn't get any printed-out statements. This is because the side effects are not produced until the sequence is consumed. It is lazy. When we actually ask for the value, the printlns will appear:

```
animal-print
;;   mouse
;; :duck
;; :dodo
;; :lory
;; :eaglet
;; -> (nil nil nil nil nil)
```

If we want to force evaluation of the side effects, we can use doall:

```
(def animal-print  (doall (map #(println %) animals)))
;;   mouse
;; :duck
;; :dodo
;; :lory
;; :eaglet
;; -> #'user/animal-print

animal-print
;; -> (nil nil nil nil nil)
```

map can also take more than one collection to map against. If more than one collection is specified, it uses each collection as a parameter to the function. For example, if we have a new function, with two parameters, which takes the keyword of the animal and a color, the map will look like this:

```
(def animals
  ["mouse" "duck" "dodo" "lory" "eaglet"])

(def colors
  ["brown" "black" "blue" "pink" "gold"])
```

```
(defn gen-animal-string [animal color]
  (str color "-" animal))

(map gen-animal-string animals colors)
;; -> ("brown-mouse" "black-duck"
;;     "blue-dodo" "pink-lory" "gold-eaglet")
```

The map function will terminate when the shortest collection ends. So if we had only two colors in our color collection, while having five animals in our animals collection, we would only end up with a two-item result:

```
(def animals
  ["mouse" "duck" "dodo" "lory" "eaglet"])

(def colors
  ["brown" "black"])

(map gen-animal-string animals colors)
;; -> ("brown-mouse" "black-duck")
```

Because the map function terminates at the shortest collection, we can even use an infinite list with it. Here is the example using a lazy color cycle:

```
(def animals
  ["mouse" "duck" "dodo" "lory" "eaglet"])

(map gen-animal-string animals (cycle ["brown" "black"]))
;; -> ("brown-mouse" "black-duck" "brown-dodo"
;;     "black-lory" "brown-eaglet")
```

Now that you can use maps, we are ready to cover one of the most important functions in Clojure, reduce.

Reduce the Ultimate

The reduce form is one of the most important fundamental building blocks of the language. It differs from map in that you can change the shape of the result as you process through the collection. A simple example of this is summing a vector of numbers:

```
(reduce + [1 2 3 4 5])
;; -> 15
```

We have taken a vector as our input shape and turned it into a single integer for the output result. More generally, reduce takes a function of two arguments: the ongoing result and the element that it is processing. Here, we are squaring the element before adding it to the ongoing total. It uses the first element of the collection as its initial value for the function:

```
(reduce (fn [r x] (+ r (* x x))) [1 2 3])
;; -> 14
```

We could change the incoming vector into a different shaped vector as well by specifying an initial value for the result before processing the first element. In this example, we are taking an animal vector and transforming it into a different vector that
doesn't include nils:

```
(reduce (fn [r x] (if (nil? x) r (conj r x)))
        []
        [:mouse nil :duck nil nil :lory])
;; -> [:mouse :duck :lory]
```

Unlike map, you cannot reduce an infinite sequence (e.g., range). The reason is that
reduce will run until one of the input collections is empty. It cannot determine the
end of an infinite sequence!

Both map and reduce are fundamental expressions that we use to shape data in Clojure. They are both abstractions built upon recursion. But we will see next that there
are other abstractions for collection processing. We will take a look at a few of the
most useful ones.

Other Useful Data Shaping Expressions

We saw we could change the incoming animal vector to a new one by filtering out
elements that were nil. There is a filter that can handle this more elegantly. It takes
a predicate and a collection as an argument.

As a predicate we are going to use the complement function that takes the function
and returns a function that takes the same arguments, but returns the opposite truth
value:

```
((complement nil?) nil)
;; -> false

((complement nil?) 1)
;; -> true
```

Now, we can use it in our filter:

```
(filter (complement nil?) [:mouse nil :duck nil])
;; -> (:mouse :duck)
```

We could even be more explicit about it by asking only for the keyword elements:

```
(filter keyword? [:mouse nil :duck nil])
;; -> (:mouse :duck)
```

There is also a remove, in case you want to specify it that way. It also takes a predicate
and a collection. We could have removed the nils from the animal vector with it as
well:

```
(remove nil? [:mouse nil :duck nil])
;; -> (:mouse :duck)
```

`for` is very useful. It allows us to specify bindings for the element in the collections that we want to process and then process the body of the function. The following example takes a vector of animals. It binds a var named `animal` to each element of the vector as it processes the body. The result is a lazy sequence of the string names of the animal. Here, we are also using the `name` function to convert a keyword to a string:

```
(for [animal [:mouse :duck :lory]]
  (str (name animal)))
;; -> ("mouse" "duck" "lory")
```

If more than one collection is specified in the `for`, it will iterate over them in a nested fashion. So, if we add a vector of colors to iterate over as well, we can have the result be a list of the combined color and animal name:

```
(for [animal [:mouse :duck :lory]
      color  [:red :blue]]
  (str (name color) (name animal)))
;; -> ("redmouse" "bluemouse"
;;     "redduck" "blueduck"
;;     "redlory" "bluelory")
```

There are also some very nice support modifiers available in `for`. One is the `:let` modifier. This allows us to specify let bindings concisely within for:

```
(for [animal [:mouse :duck :lory]
      color  [:red :blue]
      :let  [animal-str (str "animal-"(name animal))
             color-str (str "color-"(name color))
             display-str (str animal-str "-" color-str)]]
  display-str)
;; -> ("animal-mouse-color-red" "animal-mouse-color-blue"
;;     "animal-duck-color-red" "animal-duck-color-blue"
;;     "animal-lory-color-red" "animal-lory-color-blue")
```

The other support modifier is the `:when` modifier. This allows the expression to be evaluated only if the predicate is true:

```
(for [animal [:mouse :duck :lory]
      color  [:red :blue]
      :let  [animal-str (str "animal-"(name animal))
             color-str (str "color-"(name color))
             display-str (str animal-str "-" color-str)]
      :when (= color :blue)]
  display-str)
;; -> ("animal-mouse-color-blue"
;;     "animal-duck-color-blue"
;;     "animal-lory-color-blue")
```

`flatten` is another very handy and simple function. It takes any nested collection and returns the contents in a single flattened sequence:

```
(flatten [ [:duck [:mouse] [[:lory]]]])
;; -> (:duck :mouse :lory)
```

What if we want to change the form of the data structure? For example, what if we have a list and we want a vector instead? There are a couple of ways to do this. We could just use vec, but there is also into that takes the new collection and returns all the items of the collection conj-ed on to it:

```
(vec '(1 2 3))
;; -> [1 2 3]

(into [] '(1 2 3))
;; -> [1 2 3]
```

It can work with transforming maps into sorted-maps. Sorted maps are just like regular maps except there is an order to them. The key-value pairs are sorted by the keys:

```
(sorted-map :b 2 :a 1 :z 3)
;; -> {:a 1, :b 2, :z 3}
```

So we can take a regular map and turn it into a sorted-map:

```
(into (sorted-map) {:b 2 :c 3 :a 1})
;; -> {:a 1, :b 2, :c 3}
```

Or vectors of pairs into maps:

```
(into {} [[:a 1] [:b 2] [:c 3]])
;; -> {:a 1, :b 2, :c 3}
```

Or even maps into vector pairs:

```
(into [] {:a 1, :b 2, :c 3})
;; -> [[:c 3] [:b 2] [:a 1]]
```

Clojure's partition is useful for dividing up collections—for example, if we want to partition a collection into lists of three elements:

```
(partition 3 [1 2 3 4 5 6 7 8 9])
;; -> ((1 2 3) (4 5 6) (7 8 9))
```

What if the list was not evenly divisible by three?

```
(partition 3 [1 2 3 4 5 6 7 8 9 10])
;; -> ((1 2 3) (4 5 6) (7 8 9))
```

By default, partition only partitions up to the point where there are enough elements to fufill the last partition. In this case, the number 10 gets dropped off. This might be what we want, but in cases that we want to return the extra elements at the end of the partition, we should use partition-all:

```
(partition-all 3 [1 2 3 4 5 6 7 8 9 10])
;; -> ((1 2 3) (4 5 6) (7 8 9) (10))
```

There is also another function called `partition-by` that takes a function and applies it to every element in the collection. It creates a new partition every time the result changes:

```
(partition-by #(= 6 %) [1 2 3 4 5 6 7 8 9 10])
;; -> ((1 2 3 4 5) (6) (7 8 9 10))
```

We have taken a whirlwind tour through Clojure. In addition to being able to structure Clojure expressions now, you can make it dance. You can control the flow of the code through logical tests. You can make it flow back into itself with recursion. You can process only what you need with laziness. Finally, you can shape your data structures with the beauty of functional transformations.

It was a lot to take in. Don't worry if it all hasn't clicked into place yet. It will, as you continue on your tour of Clojure and with the training program in Part II. But let's forge on and take a look at how to manage state and concurrency in addition to your new Clojure code-shaping skills.

CHAPTER 3

State and Concurrency

Let's think about state.

So far we have handled things in a purely functional style. Vars, like when we were using def and defn, were global and immutable. And bindings in a let form stayed in the let form. This functional style is beautiful and lets us write cleaner and more understandable code, but we still need to deal with the real world. And the real world has state. Luckily, Clojure has a solution for us.

Handling Real-World State and Concurrency

State is messy. In most object-oriented langauges, state gets so tangled up in the code that it becomes really hard to understand what is going on. If you then have to take *all* that complexity and try to do concurrent programming on it, it quickly becomes a disaster. Clojure has a way around this. Its concurrency flows naturally from its key combination of functional style and immmutable data structures. Let's dive in and start exploring it with the humble Clojure *atom*.

Using Atoms for Independent Items

Atoms are designed to store the state of something that is *independent*, meaning we can change the value of it independently of changing any other state.

Alice is currently exploring Wonderland and just met a curious caterpillar that is sitting upon a mushroom. It isn't a giant caterpillar. Rather, it is Alice that is still small.

Let's create an atom called who-atom with the initial value of :caterpillar. We can create one using a def form and the atom form. The atom form creates a new atom and sets the value to the argument:

```
(def who-atom (atom :caterpillar))
```

If we look at the atom in the REPL, we get back the atom itself. To see the value of the atom at this moment, we need to *dereference* it with a preceding @:

```
who-atom
;; -> #<Atom@e6df69d: :caterpillar>

@who-atom
;; -> :caterpillar
```

There are a couple of ways that we can change the value of an atom. These changes are always made synchronously. The first is using `reset!`. This simply replaces the old value with the new value and returns the new value. Note that exclamation point at the end. It is idiomatic in Clojure to use it to indicate that a function changes state:

```
(reset! who-atom :chrysalis)
;; -> :chrysalis

@who-atom
;; -> :chrysalis
```

The other way is with `swap!`. The `swap!` form applies a function on the old value of the atom and sets it to the new value. In the following example, we again have an atom named `who-atom` that is initially set to the value `:caterpillar`. We then define a function that takes the state as an argument. It will change the state to the stages of a caterpillar becoming a butterfly. When we call `swap!` on the atom, it applies the function on the atom's current value and sets the value to the result of the function:

```
(def who-atom (atom :caterpillar))
```

At first, when we deref the atom, it is in the beginning state of `:caterpillar` that we initialized it to:

```
@who-atom
;; -> :caterpillar
```

We then define a `change` function. This function is going to take the current state of the atom and return a new updated value. It uses a `case` function that matches on the state. If the state is `:caterpillar`, then it will return `:chrysalis`. If the state is `:chrysalis`, it will return `butterfly`. Finally, if the state is anything else, it will return `:butterfly`. Remember that the `case` is comparing the state for equality with the first item and returning the second item on a match:

```
(defn change [state]
  (case state
    :caterpillar :chrysalis
    :chrysalis :butterfly
    :butterfly))
```

We then call the `swap!` function with the atom and the `change` function that we want to apply on the atom's value:

```
(swap! who-atom change)
;; -> :chrysalis
```

Let's check to make sure that the atom really got updated by dereferencing it:

```
@who-atom
;; -> :chrysalis
```

It indeed got updated. If we call the swap! again with the function:

```
(swap! who-atom change)
;; -> :butterfly
```

This time the case function matches on :chrysalis and returns the key :butterfly for the new value. We can check the new atom value:

```
@who-atom
;; -> :butterfly
```

We can go ahead and do this one more time:

```
(swap! who-atom change)
;; -> :butterfly
```

This time, the case function used the default return value of :butterfly to update the value. There are no more changes after the butterfly stage. Indeed, when we check the atom, it is set to :butterfly:

```
@who-atom
;; -> :butterfly
```

Something to keep in mind when using swap! is that the function used must be free of side effects. This comes in with using concurrency. The swap! operator reads the value of the atom and applies the function on it, and then compares the current value of the atom again to make sure that another thread hasn't changed it in the meantime before setting the value to the result of the function. If the value has changed in the meantime, it will retry. This means any side effects in functions might be executed multiple times.

Why does swap! behave like this? To ensure that the operation we are performing is atomic, so that other threads do not see inconsistent values. When dereferencing an atom, we always see either the value before applying the function or the result after applying the function. It is also worth noting that dereferencing the atom will never block or interfere with the operations.

Let's look at an example of this. In the first example, we are going to have an atom named counter. We are going to assign it an inital value of 0. Then we are going to use dotimes, which takes a form and executes a number of times for side effects, and execute a swap! on our counter to increment it:

```
(def counter (atom 0))

@counter
;; -> 0

(dotimes [_ 5] (swap! counter inc))❶

@counter
;; -> 5
```

❶ The underscore here is the name of the value, but we are not really using it. A convention for naming a parameter you are not using is to use an underscore.

This is fine. But we just have one thread. What if we introduce multiple threads doing this at the same time? First, how do we do things concurrently? We don't need to manipulate threads directly in Clojure. One way is to use the future form. The future form takes a body and executes it in another thread. Now we can have multiple threads incrementing the same value concurrently. We start off three threads using:

```
(def counter (atom 0))

@counter
;; -> 0

(let [n 5]
  (future (dotimes [_ n] (swap! counter inc)))
  (future (dotimes [_ n] (swap! counter inc)))
  (future (dotimes [_ n] (swap! counter inc))))

@counter
;; -> 15
```

What if we introduce a side effect in the function that we are using with swap!? Let's define a function that prints the current value of the counter before incrementing it:

```
(def counter (atom 0))

(defn inc-print [val]
  (println val)
  (inc val))

(swap! counter inc-print)
;; 0
;; -> 1
```

Now if we try to do our three threads with printing, we will see the extra print lines from when the swap! needed to retry because of another thread modifying the value before it could set it. Instead of incrementing five times for each thread each, let's just increment two times:

```
(def counter (atom 0))

(let [n 2]
  (future (dotimes [_ n] (swap! counter inc-print)))
  (future (dotimes [_ n] (swap! counter inc-print)))
  (future (dotimes [_ n] (swap! counter inc-print))))

;; 0
;; 1
;; 2
;; 2  ❶
;; 3
;; 4
;; 5

@counter
;; -> 6
```

❶   Whoa! The number 2 printed out twice!

We can see that the number 2 printed out twice; this is from the swap! retrying. Even with three threads going, the incrementing of the value was consistent and atomic. Yay for Clojure concurrency! Just remember to keep your swap! functions side-effect free.

> The code might print differently for you depending on how the threads are executed.

We just saw that atoms were used for independent and synchronous state changes. What if we have more than one thing that needs to change in a coordinated fashion? Take as an example transferring money between two bank accounts. This is where Clojure's *refs* come in. They allow this coordinated shared state. What makes them different from atoms is that you need to change their values within a transaction. Clojure uses something called *software transactional memory (STM)* to accomplish this. Refs use this STM to coordinate changes of state.

Using Refs for Coordinated Changes

All actions on refs within the transaction are:

Atomic
> Within the transaction, the updates will occur to all the refs, or if something goes wrong, none of them will be updated.

Consistent

An optional validator function can be used with the refs to check value before the transaction commits.

Isolated

A transaction has its own isolated view of the world. If another transaction is also running at the same time, the current transaction will not see any effects from it.

This might sound familiar. This is the same strategy that many databases take to coordinate transactional changes. The happy outcome of this is concurrency. The world doesn't need to stop and block other threads while changes are being made. Each transaction has everything in its own world view snapshot, to complete its transaction.

Let's see an example from *Alice in Wonderland*. The caterpillar tells Alice that eating a bit of the righthand side of the mushroom will make her bigger, while eating a bit of the lefthand side of the mushroom will make her smaller. The amount of mushroom she has in each hand is directly related to how big she is. Let's define some refs to model this. We will have two refs. One will be the height of Alice (in inches), and the other one will be the number of bites she has in her right hand:

```
(def alice-height (ref 3))
(def right-hand-bites (ref 10))
```

Just like atoms, we need to dereference them with a preceding @ to get the value:

```
@alice-height
;; -> 3

@right-hand-bites
;; -> 10
```

Let's define a function that will increment Alice's height by 24 inches for every bite she takes from the right hand. We are going to use the `alter` form, which takes a ref and a function to apply to the current value (very similar to `swap!` with atoms):

```
(defn eat-from-right-hand []
  (when (pos? @right-hand-bites)
    (alter right-hand-bites dec)
    (alter alice-height #(+ % 24))))
```

If we try to evaluate this function, we will get an error:

```
(eat-from-right-hand)
;; -> IllegalStateException No transaction running
```

We need to run this in a transaction. We do this by using a `dosync` form. This will coordinate any state changes within the form in a transaction:

```
(dosync (eat-from-right-hand))
;; -> 27
```

```
@alice-height
;; -> 27

@right-hand-bites
;; -> 9
```

Let's modify the eat-from-right-hand function slightly by moving the dosync transaction into it. While we are at it, let's test out concurrency by having three different
threads all calling the function two times:

```
(def alice-height (ref 3))   ❶
(def right-hand-bites (ref 10))

(defn eat-from-right-hand []
  (dosync (when (pos? @right-hand-bites)   ❷
            (alter right-hand-bites dec)   ❸
            (alter alice-height #(+ % 24)))))

(let [n 2]
  (future (dotimes [_ n] (eat-from-right-hand)))   ❹
  (future (dotimes [_ n] (eat-from-right-hand)))
  (future (dotimes [_ n] (eat-from-right-hand))))


@alice-height   ❺
;; -> 147

@right-hand-bites   ❻
;; -> 4
```

❶ We create two refs for alice-height and right-hand-bites. Each has initial
values.

❷ To change the values of the refs, we wrap our changes in a dosync.

❸ Here we are changing the values of both the values of the refs within the
transaction.

❹ To test out our changes, we create different threads with the *future* function,
where we call each function two times in each thread.

❺ Her final height is correct even though we had concurrent threads going on.

❻ Here, the final number of right-hand-bites left is correct.

Whoa! Did you see that? Coordinated concurrent changes just *worked*. In a real application, like a banking application, you can have multiple credits and debits happening
and not worry about the account balance getting messed up.

The function of the alter must be side-effect free, just like the swap! should be. The reason is the same: there could be retries.

There is another function called commute that we could use instead of alter. It must be called in a transaction, just like alter, and also takes a *ref* and a function. The difference between them is that commute will not retry during the transaction. Instead, it will use an *in-transaction-value* in the meantime, finally setting the *ref* value at the commit point in the transaction. This feature is very nice for speed and limiting retries. On the other hand, the function that commute applied must be *commutative* (where the order of the operands does not matter, like addition), or have a last-one-in-wins behavior. We can take a look at our last example with commute instead:

```
(def alice-height (ref 3))
(def right-hand-bites (ref 10))

(defn eat-from-right-hand []
  (dosync (when (pos? @right-hand-bites)
            (commute right-hand-bites dec)      ❶
            (commute alice-height #(+ % 24)))))

(let [n 2]
  (future (dotimes [_ n] (eat-from-right-hand)))
  (future (dotimes [_ n] (eat-from-right-hand)))
  (future (dotimes [_ n] (eat-from-right-hand))))

@alice-height
;; -> 147

@right-hand-bites
;; -> 4
```

❶ Using commute instead of alter.

Transactions that involve time-consuming computations and a large number of refs are more likely to be retried. If you are looking to limit retries, this is a reason you might prefer an *atom* with a map of state over many *refs*.

Let's try one more exercise before we move on. In this, let's have *y* always be the value of x + 2. We are going to be using ref-set instead of alter to reset the value of *y*. This is important whenever you have one ref that is defined in relation to another. Whenever you have data calculated one off of another, you can use it:

```
(def x (ref 1))  ❶
(def y (ref 1))

(defn new-values []
  (dosync  ❷
    (alter x inc)  ❸
    (ref-set y  (+ 2 @x))))  ❹

(let [n 2]
  (future (dotimes [_ n] (new-values)))  ❺
  (future (dotimes [_ n] (new-values))))

@x  ❻
;; -> 5

@y  ❼
;; -> 7
```

❶   The refs x and y are created and set to initial values.

❷   Because we are working with refs, we need to wrap our updates in a dosync transaction.

❸   We use alter on x to change its value with the inc function.

❹   For y, we directly set the new value with ref-set.

❺   Using future to create a new thread, we execute the new-values function two times each. This means the function will be called for a total of four times.

❻   The new value of x is 5.

❼   The new value of y is 7.

You can do synchronous changes now with atoms and refs, but what if you really don't care about waiting around for the answer? What if you just want to fire off your work and have it do its own thing? This is where *agents* come in.

Using Agents to Manage Changes on Their Own

Clojure atoms are used for independent synchronous changes, and refs are used for coordinated synchronous changes—now we are going to take a look at *agents*. Clojure agents are used for independent and asynchronous changes. So, basically, if there is work to be done, and you don't need the results right away, you can hand it off to an agent for processing.

Let's create an agent, this time for the capterpillar's state. The creation is very similar to the atom. We give it an initial state with a parameter:

```
(def who-agent (agent :caterpillar))
```

Then, to get the agent's value, we must dereference it:

```
@who-agent
;; -> :caterpillar
```

We can change the state of an agent by using send. The *send* form takes a function to send to the agent. This function takes the current state of the agent as an argument, along with any additional arguments you would like to define. The change function that we used earlier with the caterpillar's state with the atom's swap!, should work just fine in this case:

```
(def who-agent (agent :caterpillar))   ❶

(defn change [state]   ❷
  (case state
    :caterpillar :chrysalis
    :chrysalis :butterfly
    :butterfly))

(send who-agent change)   ❸
;; -> #<Agent@31c89c8b>

@who-agent   ❹
;; -> :chrysalis
```

❶ We create the agent with the initial value set to :caterpillar.

❷ The change function takes a state as an argument and then uses it in a case function. If the state is :caterpillar, then it will return :chrysalis. If the state is :chrysalis, it will return :butterfly. The default case will return :butterfly.

❸ The agent is sent the change function, which evaluates using the agent's current value. The agent's new value will become the result of the function.

❹ When dereferenced, the new value of the agent has been updated. Note that this happens asynchronously, so when you deref it, the value *may* be :chrysalis or not depending on the timing. However, in the case of doing it in the REPL, human time is slow enough that it will most likely be :chrysalis.

The send dispatches the action to the agent, which gets processed by a thread in the thread pool. The agent will only process one action at a time. In this respect, the agents are almost like a pipeline. The actions will be also processed in the same order that they were dispatched, if they were dispatched from the same thread. Unlike `swap!` and `alter`, send returns immediately.

Using send might not be enough if you are doing things like writing to a logfile that might block on I/O. There is another way to dispatch an action to the agent as well, with `send-off`. The `send-off` form is the same as the send form; the difference is that `send-off` should be used for potentially I/O-blocking actions. Using send uses a fixed thread pool, which is good for CPU-bound operations, whereas `send-off` uses an expandable thread pool necessary to avoid an I/O-bound thread pool from blocking:

```
(send-off who-agent change)
;; -> #<Agent@5a69b104:>

@who-agent
;; -> :butterfly
```

Agents can also handle transactions within their actions, so that means that we could change refs within our action, or send actions only if the transaction commits as well. What happens when the agent has an error or exception? Let's see by creating a `change-error` function that we can send to the agent:

```
(def who-agent (agent :caterpillar))

(defn change [state]
  (case state
    :caterpillar :chrysalis
    :chrysalis :butterfly
    :butterfly))

(defn change-error [state]
  (throw (Exception. "Boom!")))  ❶


(send who-agent change-error)  ❷
;; -> #<Agent@21ee68d5 FAILED:>

@who-agent  ❸
;; -> :caterpillar
```

❶ The change function for the agent is now throwing an exception whenever it is evaluated.

❷ When the function is actually sent to the agent, it shows as failed.

❸ Dereferencing the agent's state shows that it did not change from the previous value.

The agent's state did not change. Its value is still the initial state of caterpillar. The agent itself is now failed. The exception has been cached, and the next time an action is processed, the agent's error will be thrown. If we try to send the agent the good function change, we will see that cached error thrown:

```
(send-off who-agent change)
;; -> Exception Boom!  caterpillar.network/change-error (NO_SOURCE_FILE:1)
```

The agent's errors can also be inspected with agent-errors:

```
(agent-errors who-agent)
;; -> (#<Exception java.lang.Exception: Boom!>)
```

The agent will stay in this failed state until the agent is restarted with restart-agent, which clears its errors and resets the state of the agent:

```
(restart-agent who-agent :caterpillar)
;; -> :caterpillar

(send who-agent change)
;; -> #<Agent@21ee68d5>

@who-agent
;; -> :chrysalis
```

Different strategies to handle errors programatically can be defined when creating the agent with set-error-mode!. This will control how the agent responds to errors. It can be set to either :fail or :continue:

```
(set-error-mode! who-agent :continue)
```

If it is set to :continue and we assign an error handler with the set-error-handler-fn! function, the error handler will happen on an agent exception, but the agent itself will continue on without a need for a restart:

```
(defn err-handler-fn [a ex]
  (println "error " ex " value is " @a))

(set-error-handler! who-agent err-handler-fn)
```

Now, when we send the change-error function again to the agent we will see:

```
(def who-agent (agent :caterpillar))

(set-error-mode! who-agent :continue)

(set-error-handler! who-agent err-handler-fn)

(send who-agent change-error)
;; -> #<Agent@611ef20f: :caterpillar>
;; prints out
;;          error  #<Exception java.lang.Exception: Boom!>
;;          value is  :caterpillar

@who-agent
;; -> :caterpillar
```

But it will continue on without a restart for the next time:

```
(send who-agent change)
;; -> #<Agent@3a5bd2d6: :caterpillar>

@who-agent
;; -> :chrysalis
```

Agents in the real world are great for coordinating work you want to do in a separate process. An example of this could be relaying messages to other systems, logging to files in a safe, multithreaded way, or even sending commands to control robots.

We have seen *atoms*, *refs*, and *agents* in Clojure and how they work with concurrency. To sum up, Table 3-1 shows when you should use atoms, refs, and agents.

Table 3-1. State and concurrency options

Type	Communication	Coordination
Atom	Synchronous	Uncoordinated
Ref	Synchronous	Coordinated
Agent	Asynchronous	Uncoordinated

Awesome. You can now handle state and concurrency in the real world, and you can handle it *really* well. There is another practical aspect we need to talk about. Clojure is hosted on the Java virtual machine (JVM). This gives it quite a few pragmatic benefits. We will explore the interoperabilty with Java and polymorphism in the next chapter.

CHAPTER 4

Java Interop and Polymorphism

As already mentioned, Clojure runs on the Java virtual machine, and it uses this to its advantage. Not only is the JVM a production-hardened platform to run on, being a JVM language gives Clojure access to many different Java libraries as well as its own. We will look at how Clojure talks to Java classes in this chapter. We will also look at another way that it benefits from using Java classes for some types of polymorphism and how Clojure handles this polymorphism more generally as well.

First, we will explore Java interop.

Handling Interop with Java

When a new language comes into being, it faces the *library problem*. That is, to be useful in everyday situations, a language needs to do all the things that current dominant languages do. These current dominant languages have a full array of libraries that support things like parsing JSON and logging.

Clojure solved this new language library problem by running on the JVM and having interoperability with Java classes. When you use Clojure, you can use Java classes and Java libraries. Clojure builds on the strength of the production-hardened and tested JVM and existing Java libraries. In fact, many of the popular Clojure libraries in use today utilize Java libraries as fundamental building blocks. We are going to cover the most common areas that you will encounter: how to import Java libraries/classes, how to create new instances of them, and how to interact with their methods.

Don't sweat it if you don't have a Java background. We are just dipping our toes in. The water is fine here.

Clojure uses the *new* and *dot* special form to interact with Java classes, but provides more idiomatic forms that use them under the covers. We can take a look at this with one of Clojure's strings. For example, let's use the string `"caterpillar"`, which is one of the characters that Alice met in Wonderland. A string is really just a string from Java—it is a `java.lang.String`.

 A String in Java is an instance of `java.lang.String`. A string in Clojure is the exact same thing.

```
(class "caterpillar")
;; -> java.lang.String
```

We can transform this string to uppercase using the String's method `toUpperCase`.

The way to call `toUpperCase` in Java, would be to call it on the string itself with a dot:

```
String cString = new String("caterpillar");
cString.toUpperCase();
```

We do this in Clojure by using a dot followed by the object and the object's method that we wish to invoke:

```
(. "caterpillar" toUpperCase)
;; -> "CATERPILLAR"
```

There is also a shorthand dot prefix way to do the same thing by using a dot followed by the object's method that we wish to invoke:

```
(.toUpperCase "caterpillar")
;; -> "CATERPILLAR"
```

If the Java method takes arguments, they are included after the object. For example, if we wanted to find the index of the substring "pillar" using the string's `indexOf` method (which takes a character as a parameter), in Java we would do something like:

```
String c1String = new String("caterpillar");
String c2String = new String("pillar");
c1String.indexOf(c2);
```

In Clojure, the first argument is the string we want to call the method on, and the second is the argument:

```
(.indexOf "caterpillar" "pillar")
;; -> 5
```

We can create instances of Java objects with new:

```
(new String "Hi!!")
;; -> "Hi!!"
```

Another way to create an instance of a Java class from Clojure is to use a shorthand form for creation by using a dot right after the class name:

```
(String. "Hi!!")
;; -> "Hi!!"
```

What if we wanted to work with a Java object that we needed to import? Let's take an example of needing to reach in and do some interop networking with Java. In particular, we need to work with a `java.net.InetAddress` that represents an IP. How do we create one? The first thing we need to do is import the Java class. We can do this by using `:import` in the namespace with the package name and the class that we wish to import:

```
(ns caterpillar.network
  (:import (java.net InetAddress)))
```

We can now create an instance of `InetAddress`. The way to create a new `InetAddress` in Java is to use a static method called `getByName` that takes a string of the hostname and resolves the matching IP address. To execute static methods on Java classes from Clojure, we use a forward slash:

```
(InetAddress/getByName "localhost")
;; -> #<Inet4Address localhost/127.0.0.1>
```

Now we have a Java object that we act on and get a property off of with the dot notation:

```
(.getHostName (InetAddress/getByName "localhost"))
;; -> "localhost"
```

We can also use Java classes without importing them by using their fully qualified names:

```
(java.net.InetAddress/getByName "localhost")
;; -> #<Inet4Address localhost/127.0.0.1>
```

There is also a `doto` macro, which allows us to take a Java object and then act on it in succession with a list of operations. This is useful if we have a Java object that we need to mutate in a series of steps. We can show this with Java's `StringBuffer` object, which is a class that helps build strings. It takes an initial string as an argument. Then, if we call the method `append` with a string, it will change the object by adding that string to it:

```
(def sb (doto (StringBuffer. "Who ")
          (.append "are ")
          (.append "you?")))

(.toString sb)
;; -> "Who are you?"
```

This `doto` syntax is much nicer to read than the alternative nested version:

```
(def sb
  (.append
    (.append
    (StringBuffer. "Who ")
    "are ")
    "you?"))

(.toString sb)
;; -> "Who are you?"
```

Table 4-1 shows the code equivalents of using interop with Java compared to Clojure.

Table 4-1. Interop compared with Java

Java	Clojure
`"caterpillar".toUpperCase();`	`(.toUpperCase "caterpillar")`
`"caterpillar".indexOf("pillar");`	`(.indexOf "caterpillar" "pillar")`
`new String("Hi!!");`	`(new String "Hi!!")`
`new String("Hi!!");`	`(String. "Hi!!")`
`InetAddress.getByName("localhost");`	`(InetAddress/getByName "localhost")`
`host.getHostName();`	`(.getHostName host)`

The ability to use Java classes and libraries in such an easy way is a real advantage in Clojure. As the popularity of Clojure has spread, there are now more Clojure libraries than ever to choose from. For example, you can use Java classes to generate a universally unique identifier (UUID). Because they are very common in generating IDs for orders, customers, or images in computer programs, here is how you can use a UUID in your Clojure program:

```
(import 'java.util.UUID)  ❶
(UUID/randomUUID)  ❷
;; -> #uuid "f9877259-2cc1-4e5a-8c6f-8b51499cb9f8"
```

❶ Importing the Java class for UUID.

❷ Calling the method on the Java class to give us a unique and random UUID.

You now have the power to interact with Java's classes.

It is time to look at another way that Java's classes help out Clojure: *polymorphism*. We will take a closer look at the different ways Clojure achieves polymorphism next.

Practical Polymorphism

In an object-oriented language like Java, there are a large amount of types for every situation. Clojure takes another approach. It has a small amount of types and many different functions for them. However, being pragmatic, Clojure realizes that polymorphism is flexible and useful for some situations. Let's take a look at a few ways that Clojure can flex its polymorphic muscles.

If we wanted to have a function that would behave differently based on the kind of input we had, we could use a case like statement. This example uses a function called cond that behaves differently depending on whether the argument is a keyword, string, or number, and returns the caterpillar's questions to Alice:

```
(defn who-are-you [input]
  (cond
    (= java.lang.String (class input)) "String - Who are you?"   ❶
    (= clojure.lang.Keyword (class input)) "Keyword - Who are you?" ❷
    (= java.lang.Long (class input)) "Number - Who are you?"))   ❸

(who-are-you :alice)    ❹
;; -> "Keyword - Who are you?"

(who-are-you "alice")  ❺
;; -> "String - Who are you?"

(who-are-you 123)  ❻
;; -> "Number - Who are you?"

(who-are-you true)  ❼
;; -> nil
```

❶ The class input is compared, and if it is a string it will return `"String - Who are you?"`

❷ If it is a keyword, it will return `"Keyword - Who are you?"`

❸ If it is a number (class of Long), it will return `"Number - who are you?"`

❹ When called with a keyword, returns the clause that matched the keyword `class`.

❺ When called with a string, returns the clause that matched the string class.

❻ When called with a number, returns the clause that matched the number class.

❼ When called with a boolean, returns `nil` because there is no matching cond clause.

We can express this with polymorphism in Clojure with multimethods. We first need to define the multimethod and a function that specifies how it is going to *dispatch*; that is, how it is going to decide which of the following methods to use. In the case of our who-are-you function, the dispatch is going to be on the class of the input:

```
(defmulti who-are-you class) ❶

(defmethod who-are-you java.lang.String [input] ❷
  (str "String - who are you? " input))

(defmethod who-are-you clojure.lang.Keyword [input] ❸
  (str "Keyword - who are you? " input))

(defmethod who-are-you java.lang.Long [input] ❹
  (str "Number - who are you? " input))

(who-are-you :alice) ❺
;; -> "Keyword - who are you? :alice"

(who-are-you "Alice") ❻
;; -> "String - who are you? Alice"

(who-are-you 123) ❼
;; -> "Number - who are you? 123"

(who-are-you true) ❽
;; -> IllegalArgumentException No method in multimethod
;;'who-are-you' for dispatch value: class java.lang.Boolean
```

❶   We are declaring that the who-are-you function is going to be a multimethod with a single argument. The function that will be used for choosing what method to use is the class function. This class dispatch function takes only a single argument.

❷   Using defmethod, we say that if the class of the input is a String, then we will pass the original value of the input to a str function that will construct the "String - who are you .." return value.

❸   We do a similar defmethod dispatching on the Keyword class.

❹   And another defmethod dispatching on the Long class.

❺   When we call the who-are-you function with a keyword, it not only uses the method defined for keywords, it also returns the value of the :alice input in the return string.

❻ Calling with a string results in the function defined for the string class along with the "Alice" value in the return string.

❼ Calling with a number also shows that the function defined for the Long class was used along with the number 123.

❽ Calling with a boolean throws an error because it couldn't find a matching dispatch method.

We could also provide a default dispatch method using the `:default` keyword, so if we don't have a matching one it will use that instead of throwing an exception:

```
(defmethod who-are-you :default [input]
  (str "I don't know - who are you? " input))

(who-are-you true)
;; -> "I don't know - who are you? true"
```

In the previous example, the `dispatch` function is called first, which is the class of the input. Then, using that value, it decides what method to use.

Really, any function can be given to dispatch on. So, we can even inspect the value of a map as input. What if we wanted to have a multimethod to control the conversation of the caterpillar based on the value of Alice's question?

In this example, we are going to create a multimethod that is dispatched on a function of her height, so that she knows which side of the mushroom to eat from.

First, we declare that the function named `eat-mushroom` is going to be a multimethod with `defmulti`. This time, instead of using the class function, we are going to define our own. It is a function that takes a one parameter, height. If the height is less than 3, then the `:grow` keyword will be returned; otherwise, the `:shrink` keyword will be returned:

```
(defmulti eat-mushroom (fn [height]
                         (if (< height 3)
                           :grow
                           :shrink)))
```

The `:grow` and `:shrink` keywords that we are choosing to dispatch on now need `def` methods for each of them. For the `:grow` keyword, we will simply return a helpful string that tells the user to eat the right side to grow:

```
(defmethod eat-mushroom :grow [_]
  "Eat the right side to grow.")
```

Then the `:shrink` keyword will do something similar, only it will return a helpful string to eat the other side of the mushroom:

```
(defmethod eat-mushroom :shrink [_]
  "Eat the left side to shrink.")
```

 You will notice that we are using an underscore instead of using a
name for the parameter in the defmethods. This is an idiomatic
way to say that we don't care about the value of the input here—we
are not going to use it, and effectively ignore it.

When we try call the eat-mushroom function with a small height, it will tell us the
hint to grow:

```
(eat-mushroom 1)
;; -> "Eat the right side to grow."
```

```
Likewise, when we call it with a big height, it will tell us the hint to shrink.
```

```
(eat-mushroom 9)
;; -> "Eat the left side to shrink."
```

Another way to use polymorphism in Clojure is to use *protocols*. Where multimethods are great using polymorphism on one function, sometimes protocols can
handle polymorphism elegantly with groups of functions. Let's take a look at this with
the eat-mushroom example using a String, Keyword, and a Long. First, we need to
define the protocol:

```
(defprotocol BigMushroom
  (eat-mushroom [this]))
```

Next, we implement the protocol for all our types at once using extend-protocol.
The parameter this is the thing that we are going to perform the function on:

```
(extend-protocol BigMushroom
  java.lang.String
  (eat-mushroom [this]
    (str (.toUpperCase this) " mmmm tasty!"))

  clojure.lang.Keyword
  (eat-mushroom [this]
    (case this
      :grow "Eat the right side!"
      :shrink "Eat the left side!"))

  java.lang.Long
  (eat-mushroom [this]
    (if (< this 3)
      "Eat the right side to grow"
      "Eat the left side to shrink")))
```

Now, we can call the function with the data types quite naturally:

```
(eat-mushroom "Big Mushroom")
;; -> "BIG MUSHROOM mmmm tasty!"

(eat-mushroom :grow)
;; -> "Eat the right side!"

(eat-mushroom 1)
;; -> "Eat the right side to grow"
```

We have been using protocols to add methods to existing data structure. However, what if we want to add our own?

Clojure's answer to this is data types. There are two solutions depending on what you are looking for. If you need structured data, the answer is to use `defrecord`, which actually creates a class with a new type. The `defrecord` form defines the fields that the class will hold. To demonstrate, we will make a `defrecord` to describe the mushroom that the caterpillar was sitting on when Alice met him. It had a color and a height:

```
(defrecord Mushroom [color height])
;; -> caterpillar.network.Mushroom
```

Now we can create a new mushroom object with a dot notation:

```
(def regular-mushroom (Mushroom. "white and blue polka dots" "2 inches"))
;; -> #'caterpillar.network/regular-mushroom

(class regular-mushroom)
;; -> caterpillar.network.Mushroom
```

Notice that the class type that was produced was the same as the one defined by `defre cord`. We can get the values with the dot-dash that is preferred over the dot-prefix form for accessing fields:

```
(.-color regular-mushroom)
;; -> "white and blue polka dots"

(.-height regular-mushroom)
;; -> "2 inches"
```

We can combine the structured data and type that `defrecord` gives us with protocols to implement interfaces. The mushroom that Alice encountered in Wonderland was special. If she ate from one side of the mushroom it made her grow big, and the other side made her grow small. Let's define a protocol for a mushroom to be edible. Of course, it will work differently on different types of mushrooms. The protocol will be called `Edible` and it will consist of two functions: one called `bite-right-side` and one called `bite-left-side`. Each of these functions takes `this` as an argument, which is the record itself that we will call it with later:

```
(defprotocol Edible
  (bite-right-side [this])
  (bite-left-side [this]))
```

Now that we have a protocol defined, we can start having records that implement it. The type of record that we will make is a WonderlandMushroom:

```
(defrecord WonderlandMushroom [color height] ❶
  Edible ❷
  (bite-right-side [this]   ❸
    (str "The " color " bite makes you grow bigger"))
  (bite-left-side [this]   ❹
    (str "The " color " bite makes you grow smaller")))
```

❶ Creates a WonderlandMushroom record that takes arguments that set the color and height.

❷ Implements the Edible protocol.

❸ Defines the implementation for the bite-right-side function.

❹ Defines the implementation for the bite-left-side function.

Next, we define a record for a RegularMushroom. It is very similar to the Wonderland Mushroom. It has the same constructor, and implements the Edible protocol. The main difference is in what the functions do. The bites of the mushroom don't make you grow bigger or smaller. They just taste bad:

```
(defrecord RegularMushroom [color height]
  Edible
  (bite-right-side [this]
    (str "The " color " bite tastes bad"))
  (bite-left-side [this]
    (str "The " color " bite tastes bad too")))
```

Finally, we can construct our mushrooms with the record dot syntax:

```
(def alice-mushroom (WonderlandMushroom. "blue dots" "3 inches"))
(def reg-mushroom (RegularMushroom. "brown" "1 inches"))
```

When we take bites from the WonderlandMushroom, they give us the growing messages:

```
(bite-right-side alice-mushroom)
;; -> "The blue dots bite makes you grow bigger"

(bite-left-side alice-mushroom)
;; -> "The blue dots bite makes you grow smaller"
```

And when we take bites from the RegularMushroom, they taste bad:

```
(bite-right-side reg-mushroom)
;; -> "The brown bite tastes bad"

(bite-left-side reg-mushroom)
;; -> "The brown bite tastes bad too"
```

We have gone through a fun example with protocols and *Alice in Wonderland*. But we will stop for a moment to talk about when to use protocols in a practical setting.

A real-world example of protocols is implementing different types of persistence. It is common in a business setting to want to write information to a data source. The information that we write stays the same, but we are writing it to different types of data sources. We could have one defrecord type persist the result to a database and another could persist the result to an Amazon S3 bucket. We can easily adapt the same technique we used with mushrooms to store information.

In the previous example, we were using records that held structured data values. Sometimes we don't really care about the structure or the map lookup features provided by defrecord, we just need an object with a type to save memory. In this case, we should reach for deftype. We can show this using the mushroom example, except this time, we don't care what color the mushroom is, or how tall it is.

The protocol itself doesn't change:

```
(defprotocol Edible
  (bite-right-side [this])
  (bite-left-side [this]))
```

The difference is that instead of using defrecord, we are now going to use deftype:

```
(deftype WonderlandMushroom [] ❶
  Edible ❷
  (bite-right-side [this] ❸
    (str "The bite makes you grow bigger"))
  (bite-left-side [this] ❹
    (str "The bite makes you grow smaller")))
```

❶ Use deftype to define a WonderlandMushroom with no arguments.

❷ It implements the Edible protocol.

❸ The function for bite-right-side is simply a string telling you that it makes you bigger.

❹ The function for bite-left-side likewise tells you that it will make you smaller.

The RegularMushroom looks the same as the WonderlandMushroom (with less magic, of course):

```
(deftype RegularMushroom []
  Edible
  (bite-right-side [this]
    (str "The bite tastes bad"))
  (bite-left-side [this]
    (str "The bite tastes bad too")))
```

We construct the mushrooms the same way as before with the dot notation:

```
(def alice-mushroom (WonderlandMushroom.))
(def reg-mushroom (RegularMushroom.))
```

Tasting the mushrooms gives the growing response for the WonderlandMushroom and the taste bad response for the RegularMushroom:

```
(bite-right-side alice-mushroom)
;; -> "The bite makes you grow bigger"

(bite-left-side alice-mushroom)
;; -> "The bite makes you grow smaller"

(bite-right-side reg-mushroom)
;; -> "The bite tastes bad"

(bite-left-side reg-mushroom)
;; -> "The bite tastes bad too"
```

The main difference between using protocols with defrecord and deftype is how you want your data organized. If you want structured data, choose defrecord. Otherwise, use deftype. Why? Because with records, you get type-based dispatch and you can still manipulate your data like maps (which is great for reuse). Sometimes, when this structured data isn't needed, you can use deftype to avoid paying for the overhead for something you don't want.

Clojure protocols and data types are powerful solutions when you need them, but beware! Many people who come from an object-oriented background tend to reach for them and use them just because they are similar to how they are used to modeling and thinking about code.

 Think before you use protocols.

In the example we just did using protocols, we could have actually used other ways to get the same result. Instead of using a protocol, we could have used a simple map to distinguish what kind of mushroom it was.

We could define the `bite-right-side` function to take a mushroom as an argument. This argument would be a map containing a key of `:type`. If the `:type` key value is equal to the string `"wonderland"`, then we could know that it was a special mushroom that could make you grow bigger. Otherwise, it would just be considered a regular mushroom:

```
(defn bite-right-side [mushroom]  ❶
  (if (= (:type mushroom) "wonderland")
    "The bite makes you grow bigger"
    "The bite tastes bad"))
```

❶ The mushroom argument is a map with a key `:type` in it.

We could then define a similar function for the left side:

```
(defn bite-left-side [mushroom]
  (if (= (:type mushroom) "wonderland")
    "The bite makes you grow smaller"
    "The bite tastes bad too"))
```

When we bite into the wonderland mushroom, with the map key `:type` set to `"wonderland"`, it will give us the growing messages:

```
(bite-right-side {:type "wonderland"})
;; -> "The bite makes you grow bigger"

(bite-left-side {:type "wonderland"})
;; -> "The bite makes you grow smaller"
```

And of course, when we bite into the regular mushroom, it tastes bad:

```
(bite-right-side {:type "regular"})
;; -> "The bite tastes bad"

(bite-left-side {:type "regular"})
;; -> "The bite tastes bad too"
```

As you can see, there are multiple ways to get functions to behave differently based on values and types.

Protocols should be used sparingly. In most situations, a pure function or multimethod can be used instead. A nice thing about Clojure is that it is easy to move from just maps to records when you need to. This allows you to delay the decision of whether or not to use protocols.

You can now handle real-world state and concurrency with *atoms*, *refs*, and *agents*. You can also handle polymorphism in a practical way. The tools to conquer stuctured data, types, and interfaces where pure functional approaches don't work are in your hands. You have all the skills you need to start creating your own Clojure projects and explore the ecosystem in the next chapter.

CHAPTER 5

How to Use Clojure Projects and Libraries

Over the past few chapters, you have grown strong in your Clojure knowledge. You now know the fundamentals of the language, how to shape and control code in a functional way, and how to interact with the real world. So far, we have been working with short code snippets in a stand-alone REPL. Now, we will start building a project with Clojure.

In this chapter, we are going to be creating a Clojure project using the Leiningen build tool. Along the way, we are going to learn about how to run Clojure programs and test them, as well as how to manage and use libraries in our project.

Because we are going to be working with files and a directory structure, you might be wondering: What editor do I use for Clojure?

Getting Set Up with a Clojure Editor

There are many different choices for editors today. The best one for you is quite a subjective decision. It is wise, however, to try not to learn too many things at once. Try to use an editor or plug-in that you already know. Later, after you become more comfortable with Clojure, experiment with other editors and see what you like best. Here are a few of the most common editors/plug-ins for Clojure:

IntelliJ

There is a very nice plug-in for the ItelliJ editor (*http://www.jetbrains.com/idea/*) called Cursive (*https://cursiveclojure.com/userguide/*). It has quite a few good editing features for Clojure.

Eclipse

The Eclipse editor (*https://www.eclipse.org/*) also has a good plug-in called CounterClockwise (*http://doc.ccw-ide.org/*). It has good, solid Clojure support.

Vim

> If you are a vim user, you should check out Fireplace (*https://github.com/tpope/vim-fireplace*) for your REPL needs.

Emacs

> Emacs is a wonderful editor for Clojure code. It is also not just an editor—it is a *lifestyle*. This is the one you should try once you feel comfortable in the Clojure world. The Cider package (*https://github.com/clojure-emacs/cider*) provides a wonderful coding experience. I use Emacs because it has good integration with REPL and easily evaluates individual expressions without the weight of a bigger IDE.
>
> Although again, don't try to learn Emacs at the same time as a new language. It is really hard. Consider trying to pick it up after you have some experience with Clojure.

Light Table

> If you didn't see your favorite editor mentioned, I would give Light Table (*http://www.lighttable.com/*) a try. It is an integrated editor that is very easy to use and set up and has excellent Clojure and REPL support. This is the one you should use if you are just starting out.

So, take a few minutes and pick your editor, visit the website listed, and set it up. Our next step will be to create a project for it to use.

Creating Our Project with Leiningen

We created a project with Leiningen back in the very beginning of the book. However, we just used it to run the Clojure REPL and to explore the Clojure examples in the chapters. Although you can use Clojure with other build systems like Maven, Leiningen is the best, most friendly way. You can create projects and download dependencies with a simple command. It is also well documented and maintained, and is the most common way to manage projects in the Clojure ecosystem.

Let's use Leiningen to create a brand-new project and explore the file structure and configuration.

We need a theme for our project, so let's check on Alice's adventures. In Chapter 4, she met with a caterpillar that told her to eat some of the mushroom to change her size, because she was really small. She sampled the mushroom and immediately began to grow at an alarming rate. Her head rocketed up into the top of the trees where she met a pigeon that screamed, "Serpent!"

Let's name our project *serpent-talk*. To get started, open a command prompt and type the following:

```
lein new serpent-talk
```

Now go into the new project that you just created and take a look by using the following command:

```
cd serpent-talk
```

You should see that it created a directory structure that looks like:

```
.
├── LICENSE
├── README.md
├── doc
│   └── intro.md
├── project.clj
├── resources
├── src
│   └── serpent_talk
│       └── core.clj
└── test
    └── serpent_talk
        └── core_test.clj
6 directories, 6 files
```

Let's now discuss the purpose of each of these files:

LICENSE
> The default generated license for the project is the Eclipse Public License, which is suitable for most open source work.

README.md
> This is a skeleton for a Markdown information page about our project. It provides a title, a section to fill out about what our project does, and other sections for usage and license.

doc/intro.md
> This is a template to encourage us to document our project for others-always a worthwhile endeavor.

project.clj
> This is the main configuration file for our project and all its dependencies.

resources
> This is the directory to keep any extra files (like an image) our program might need.

src/serpent_talk/core.clj
> This is our main Clojure code file. Notice how the directory name *serpent_talk* uses underscores even though the project name uses hyphens *(serpent-talk)*. This is important and we will talk about it more in a minute.

test/serpent_talk/core_test.clj

This is our automatically generated test file for our main core code file.

Leiningen automatically generated our code files with the name *core.clj* and *core-test.clj*. However, it is much better to give the files some meaningful name *other* than core. So the first thing that we will do is rename them to *talk.clj* and *talk-test.clj*.

Go ahead and do the following:

1. Rename *src/serpent_talk/core.clj* to *src/serpent_talk/talk.clj*.

2. Rename *test/serpent_talk/core_test.clj* to *test/serpent_talk/talk_test.clj*.

The files should now have the following directory structure:

```
├── LICENSE
├── README.md
├── doc
│   └── intro.md
├── project.clj
├── resources
├── src
│   └── serpent_talk
│       └── talk.clj
└── test
    └── serpent_talk
        └── talk_test.clj
6 directories, 6 files
```

Now, use your editor of choice and open the *src/serpent_talk/talk.clj* file. You should see the code that Leiningen has automatically generated for us. This is the basic template that Leiningen will generate for you whenever you run the **lein new** command:

```
(ns serpent-talk.core)

(defn foo
  "I don't do a whole lot."
  [x]
  (println x "Hello, World!"))
```

Where did the function foo come from? It was autogenerated for us by Leiningen. Just a nice stub function to get us started.

The function foo in the file is just a placeholder. The string "I don't do a whole lot", is called a *doc-string*. It helps annotate and describe your functions for people using your project, and of course yourself.

The namespace of the file is the project name (with hyphens), followed by the filename. Here we need to make a slight change because we renamed the file to *talk.clj*. We need to change the namespace to match the new *talk* filename.

Go ahead and change

```
(ns serpent-talk.core)
```

to

```
(ns serpent-talk.talk)
```

We saw that the file directory is actually created with underscores rather than hyphens. This is so that the Clojure file compiles properly. The nitty-gritty details have to do with dashes not being valid in Java class names, but for now, just remember that the filename uses underscores, while the namespace uses dashes.

 Always use underscores for directories and filenames, and use dashes for namespaces.

Next, let's take a look at the test file that it generated for us. Open the *test/ serpent_talk/talk_test.clj* file. You should see the following code:

```
(ns serpent-talk.core-test
  (:require [clojure.test :refer :all]
            [serpent-talk.core :refer :all]))

(deftest a-test
  (testing "FIXME, I fail."
    (is (= 0 1))))
```

The first thing to notice is the namespace. Because we changed the filename to *talk_test.clj*, we need to change the namespace to match it.

Go ahead and change

```
(ns serpent-talk.core-test
  (:require [clojure.test :refer :all]
            [serpent-talk.core :refer :all]))
```

to

```
(ns serpent-talk.talk-test ❶
  (:require [clojure.test :refer :all]
            [serpent-talk.talk :refer :all])) ❷
```

❶ Change the namespace to match our filename.

❷ We are importing the source file so we need to change *serpent-talk.core* to *serpent-talk.talk* to match our renamed file.

Now, look at the test portion of the file. You will see a `deftest` function here is also an autogenerated template from Leiningen:

```
(deftest a-test  ❶
  (testing "FIXME, I fail."  ❷
    (is (= 0 1))))  ❸
```

There are a few things to point out about the test file that Leiningen generated for us.
First is to notice what files are included in the namespace. There are two namespaces
that are being used. The *clojure.test* library is being loaded with the keywords :refer
and :all. This means that all the functions and symbols in the test library can be
used in the *serpent-talk.talk-test* namespace without having to qualify the namespace.
This is important because it uses deftest, testing, and is to create the sample test.

❶   deftest defines a test function.

❷   testing is used within deftest to provide a context to what is being tested.

❸   is provides the assertion that is being tested.

The other namespace that is being loaded is the main namespace the test file is
responsible for testing. In this case, it is the *serpent-talk.talk* namespace. It is also
doing a :refer and :all to have the test refer to the symbols directly.

This test is not doing very much right now. Leiningen provides a skeleton with a failing test to get you started. We can run the tests. Depending on what editor you are
using, you may be able to run the test from your editor. You can also always run the
tests from the command prompt using Leiningen.

Type in the following to run the tests:

```
-> lein test

lein test serpent-talk.talk-test

lein test :only serpent-talk.talk-test/a-test
```

You should receive the following output:

```
FAIL in (a-test) (talk_test.clj:7)
FIXME, I fail.
expected: (= 0 1)
  actual: (not (= 0 1))

Ran 1 tests containing 1 assertions.
1 failures, 0 errors.
Tests failed.
```

The test fails. The error tells us that it expected 0 to equal 1. That doesn't sound right.

Modify a-test to pass by changing the 0 to 1 so that it is true:

```
(ns serpent-talk.talk-test
  (:require [clojure.test :refer :all]
```

```
        [serpent-talk.talk :refer :all]))

(deftest a-test
  (testing "FIXME, I fail."
    (is (= 1 1)))) ❶
```

❶ Fix the failing test by making the statement true.

Run the tests again to see them pass:

```
-> lein test

lein test serpent-talk.talk-test

Ran 1 tests containing 1 assertions.
0 failures, 0 errors.
```

There is another directory in our project structure that we have not talked about yet. If you take a look, you will see that a directory called *target* was created when you ran the lein test command. This directory contains information about the compiled classes.

Here's a quick recap of the project setup before we move on:

- Run lein new serpent-talk to create a new Clojure project skeleton.

- The automatically generated source code file is found in *src/serpent_talk/core.clj*.

- The automatically generated test code file is found in *test/serpent_talk/ core_test.clj*.

- Rename the automatically generating files to a meaningful name. In our case, rename *core* to *talk*.

- To run the tests, use the command **lein test**.

Let's move on to take a closer look at the *project.clj* configuration file. Open the *project.clj* file in the root of the project. It should look like this:

```
(defproject serpent-talk "0.1.0-SNAPSHOT" ❶ ❷
  :description "FIXME: write description" ❸
  :url "http://example.com/FIXME" ❹
  :license {:name "Eclipse Public License" ❺
            :url "http://www.eclipse.org/legal/epl-v10.html"}
  :dependencies [[org.clojure/clojure "1.6.0"]]) ❻
```

This code was all autogenerated for us by Leiningen. It is also all the information about our project.

❶ *serpent-talk* is our project name

❷ *"0.1.0-SNAPSHOT"* is our initial project version

❸ The :description is just a human-readable description of what the project is

❹ The :url is a stubbed out example URL for our project

❺ The :license is kindly defaulted to the Eclipse Public License

❻ The :dependencies just has one library that our project is depending upon—Clojure

So what happens with the Clojure dependency? Where does it come from? Where does it go? We will find the answer by learning more about how Leiningen does dependency management.

Dependency Management with Leiningen

In the dependencies section of the configuration file we specified the following:

```
[org.clojure/clojure "1.6.0"]
```

This is the information that Leiningen uses to figure out what library/JAR files to search for. In particular, it uses three parts:

- group-id identifies an entity uniquely across all projects, like a domain name.
- artifact-id is the name without a version.
- version is the specific version release of the project.

 For those not familar with Java JARs, they are a way to package up Java class files and resources for distribution.

Leiningen gets this information from our dependency section in our project configuration. In the case of:

```
[org.clojure/clojure "1.6.0"]
```

- `org.clojure` is the group id
- `clojure` is the artifact id
- `1.6.0` is the version

Whenever any code from your project is run (such as during tests), Leiningen will ensure all the dependencies you've declared are downloaded from the proper artifact repositories. By default, Leiningen will check two popular open source repositories:

- Clojars (*https://clojars.org/*)
- Maven Central (*http://search.maven.org/*)

We don't need to do this here, but for reference, it can also be configured to look at additional repositories (public and private), by using the `:repositories` key in the configuration file.

Once Leiningen figures out what dependencies it needs to download, it transfers them to your local machine. By default, it stores them in your *maven* home directory. It looks something like this on a Mac/Linux system:

```
-> ls ~/.m2/repository/org/clojure/clojure/1.6.0/
_maven.repositories      clojure-1.6.0.jar        clojure-1.6.0.jar.sha1
clojure-1.6.0.pom        clojure-1.6.0.pom.sha1
```

It stores the JAR file and the associated information files in a directory structure that is defined by the group, artifact, and version. This is the JAR that your program will use to run Clojure. Another nice tool to use is `lein deps :tree`. It will show you a tree structure of the exact libraries and versions that your project is using—after all the dependencies have been resolved.

Now that we know how to configure and download dependencies with the project file, let's actually add a library to help our project do something interesting. We talked earlier about the importance of how code filenames should have underscores, while Clojure namespaces should have dashes. There are actually terms for these naming conventions. Underscore naming is referred to as *snake case* and naming with dashes is called *kebab case*. Also, from Java classes we have *camel case*. Here's an illustration of each naming convention:

- this_is_snake_case
- this-is-kebab-case
- ThisIsCamelCase

There is a nice Clojure library, with an awesome name, that handles string conversions from one naming convention to another. It is called *camel-snake-kebab*. If you go to the Clojars (*https://clojars.org/*) website, as shown in Figure 5-1, you can search for the library and find the latest revision information.

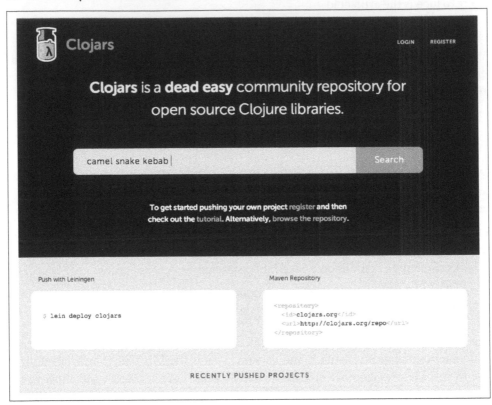

Figure 5-1. Clojars home page

The latest dependency format for Leiningen will display, along with information about previous versions. There is also a link to the GitHub repo for the project itself. An example of this in the *camel-snake-kebab* library on Clojars, as shown in Figure 5-2.

Let's modify the *project.clj* file to include this new dependency. Add the following code to the file:

```
[camel-snake-kebab "0.2.4"]
```

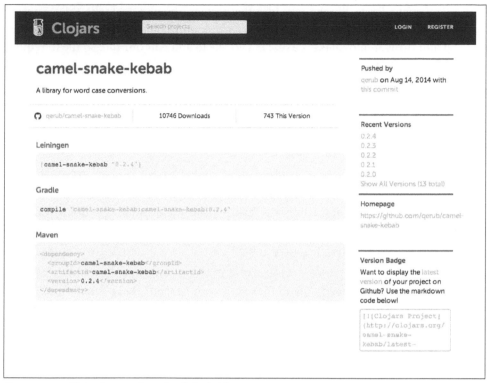

Figure 5-2. Clojar's camel-snake-kebab library

The full *project.clj* file should now look like this:

```
(defproject serpent-talk "0.1.0-SNAPSHOT"
  :description "FIXME: write description"
  :url "http://example.com/FIXME"
  :license {:name "Eclipse Public License"
            :url "http://www.eclipse.org/legal/epl-v10.html"}
  :dependencies [[org.clojure/clojure "1.6.0"]
                 [camel-snake-kebab "0.2.4"]])
```

We are ready to go and use the library in our new Clojure project.

Using Libraries in Your Own Project

In the spirit of the pigeon that yelled "Serpent!" at Alice, let's create a function that will take a string and then return the following:

```
"Serpent!  You said: "
```

followed by some transformation of the text we put into the function.

The *camel-snake-kebab* library provides the perfect function to make this happen. From its documentation, we can see there is a function called →snake_case that takes a string and turns it into snake_case. Let's go ahead and edit our *talk.clj* file to require the library and try out this function.

The file should now look like this:

```
(ns serpent-talk.talk
  (:require [camel-snake-kebab.core :as csk]))

(csk/->snake_case "hello pigeon")
```

See if you can get a REPL started with your editor in this namespace. The process is different depending on which one you are using. In Light Table, you can open the file, put the cursor at the end of the line with csk/→snake_case and hit Cmd/Ctrl-Enter to connect to the REPL and see the results:

```
(csk/->snake_case "hello pigeon")
;; -> "hello_pigeon"
```

We have everything we need now to make our own serpent-talk function. This is a perfect time to write a quick test for what we expect our great new function to do. Open the *talk_test.clj* file and let's modify it:

```
(ns serpent-talk.talk-test
  (:require [clojure.test :refer :all]
            [serpent-talk.talk :refer :all]))

(deftest test-serpent-talk
  (testing "Cries serpent! with a snake_case version of the input"
    (is (= "Serpent!  You said: hello_there"
           (serpent-talk "hello there")))))
```

Great! Run the test, either with your editor or lein test and see what happens.

Ouch—we get an error:

```
Exception in thread "main"
java.lang.RuntimeException:
Unable to resolve symbol: serpent-talk in this context
```

This is reminding us that we don't actually have a function named serpent-talk defined in our *talk.clj* file yet. Let's go ahead and add one:

```
(ns serpent-talk.talk
  (:require [camel-snake-kebab.core :as csk]))

(defn serpent-talk [input]
  (csk/->snake_case input))
```

Run the test again and see what happens.

Closer, but we are still failing:

```
-> lein test

lein test serpent-talk.talk-test

lein test :only serpent-talk.talk-test/test-serpent-talk

FAIL in (test-serpent-talk) (talk_test.clj:7)
Cries serpent! with a snake_case version of the input
expected: (= "Serpent!  You said: hello_there" (serpent-talk "hello there"))
  actual: (not (= "Serpent!  You said: hello_there" "hello_there"))

Ran 1 tests containing 1 assertions.
1 failures, 0 errors.
Tests failed.
```

We just need to add the prefix:

```
"Serpent!  You said:"
```

That is not too hard. Let's fix that in *talk.clj*:

```
(ns serpent-talk.talk
  (:require [camel-snake-kebab.core :as csk]))

(defn serpent-talk [input]
  (str "Serpent!  You said: "
       (csk/->snake_case input)))
```

Run the test one more time:

```
-> lein test it will automatically run our code.

lein test serpent-talk.talk-test

Ran 1 tests containing 1 assertions.
0 failures, 0 errors.
```

Yay! We used a library in a real Clojure project, wrote tests, and made them pass.

You might want to try adding in functions to kebab-case or camelCase on your own.

Now let's see what we can do with our little project. How about running it from the command line?

We can do this with a few simple changes. First, in our *talk.clj* file, we need to add a -main function that will get passed in the command-line arguments:

```
(defn -main [& args]
  (println (serpent-talk (first args))))
```

The [& args] in the function means a variable number of arguments can be accessed in a vector named *args*.

This will take in the first argument from the command line and then print the result of our serpent-talk function. After you have made your changes, the full *talk.clj* class should now look like this:

```clojure
(ns serpent-talk.talk
  (:require [camel-snake-kebab.core :as csk]))

(defn serpent-talk [input]
  (str "Serpent!  You said: "
       (csk/->snake_case input)))

(defn -main [& args]
  (println (serpent-talk (first args))))
```

You can now run it from the command line with lein run -m and the namespace.

Type the following in the command line:

```
-> lein run -m serpent-talk.talk "Hello pigeon"
```

Did you see the following print out on your terminal?

```
Serpent!  You said: hello_pigeon
```

We just ran the main function of our namespace from the command line using the lein run -m command. We can also modify our project so that when we simply type in lein run it will automatically run our code.

We also need to make a modification to our *project.clj* file. We need to add a :main key to point to which namespace's main function to execute when we do a lein run. It now should look like this:

```clojure
(defproject serpent-talk "0.1.0-SNAPSHOT"
  :description "FIXME: write description"
  :url "http://example.com/FIXME"
  :license {:name "Eclipse Public License"
            :url "http://www.eclipse.org/legal/epl-v10.html"}
  :dependencies [[org.clojure/clojure "1.6.0"]
                 [camel-snake-kebab "0.2.4"]]
  :main serpent-talk.talk)
```

Now type in the following:

```
lein run "Hello pigeon"
```

You will see:

```
-> lein run "Hello pigeon"
Serpent!  You said: hello_pigeon
```

You have created your own Clojure project and used a library from the Clojure ecosystem in it. We will build on what we have learned here in the next chapter as we look at using a really powerful library for asynchronous communication called *core.async*.

CHAPTER 6

Communication with core.async

Now that you know how to use libraries, you can get to know a very nice library called *core.async*, which allows asynchronous and concurrent communication through *channels*. This allows independent threads of activity to communicate with one another and is an important tool for fast processing and communication. We'll start exploring how it works with the help of Alice and a sample project.

As Alice continued on her adventure in Wonderland, she happened upon a tea party. It wasn't just a regular tea party, it was a *mad* tea party (and by *mad* I mean crazy). The Mad Hatter, March Hare, and Dormouse were at the table when Alice joined them.

To create a new project, follow these steps:

1. Run the following command:

   ```
   lein new async-tea-party
   ```

2. Go into the new directory that was created:

   ```
   cd async-tea-party
   ```

Now that you have the project created, you need to modify the *project.clj* file to include the *core.async* library. You can go to the GitHub project page for core.async (*https://github.com/clojure/core.async*) to check for the latest version. It will look something like Figure 6-1.

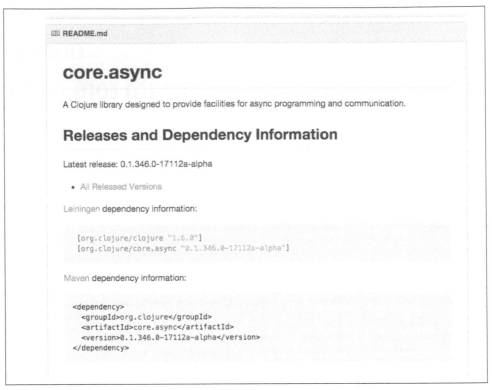

Figure 6-1. GitHub core-async

Edit your *project.clj* file to include the correct dependency info for the latest *core-async* library:

```
(defproject async-tea-party "0.1.0-SNAPSHOT"
  :description "FIXME: write description"
  :url "http://example.com/FIXME"
  :license {:name "Eclipse Public License"
            :url "http://www.eclipse.org/legal/epl-v10.html"}
  :dependencies [[org.clojure/clojure "1.6.0"]
                 [org.clojure/core.async "0.1.346.0-17112a-alpha"]])
```

Open up the *src/async_tea_party/core.clj* file, include the *core.async* library in the namespace, and delete the template foo function. The full edited file should look like this:

```
(ns async-tea-party.core
  (:require [clojure.core.async :as async]))
```

Get your REPL up and running. We are ready to start coding our async tea party. Before we get to our final code, we are going to have to learn a few things about how to work with channels and the async library. First, we will work through some examples in the REPL. Then, when we have the basics, we can create our final functions.

Basics of core.async Channels

The basics are learning how to create channels, and get values on and off of the channels. First, create a channel. Luckily, this is quite a simple thing to do. Let's practice in the REPL before building a working code example:

```
(def tea-channel (async/chan))
```

This created a simple channel we can put things on, like tea. There are two main ways that you get things on and off channels: synchronously and asynchronously. Let's start with the synchronous way, with blocking puts and takes:

- A blocking put is indicated by >!!. It puts data on the channel synchronously.
- A blocking take is indicated by <!!. It takes data off the channel synchronously.

We can start off by putting a cup of tea on the tea-channel. The only problem is that our tea-channel is *unbuffered* right now. So if we were to try to put a value on the channel, the main thread would block until it got taken off. Unfortunately, it would also lock up our REPL and program. We can solve this by creating a buffered tea-channel instead, by specifying the size of the buffer as we create it. Now, *puts* to this channel (with a fixed buffer) will not block the thread unless the buffer is full:

```
(def tea-channel (async/chan 10))
```

Now we can put our cup of tea on the tea-channel with the blocking put:

```
(async/>!! tea-channel :cup-of-tea)
;; -> true
```

 When you see !! it means a blocking call.

We can get it off again with a blocking take:

```
(async/<!! tea-channel)
;; -> :cup-of-tea
```

We can close our tea-channel with close!. This closes the channel to new inputs; however, if there are still values on it, they can be taken off. When the channel is finally empty, it will return a nil. Let's put some more cups of tea on the tea-channel and then close it:

```
(async/>!! tea-channel :cup-of-tea-2)
;; -> true
(async/>!! tea-channel :cup-of-tea-3)
;; -> true
```

```
(async/>!! tea-channel :cup-of-tea-4)
;; -> true

(async/close! tea-channel)
;; -> nil
```

What happens when we try to put another cup of tea on the closed channel?

```
(async/>!! tea-channel :cup-of-tea-5)
;; -> false
```

It returns false because it has been closed. Can we take our cups of tea off the channel that we already put on there?

```
(async/<!! tea-channel)
;; -> :cup-of-tea-2

(async/<!! tea-channel)
;; -> :cup-of-tea-3

(async/<!! tea-channel)
;; -> :cup-of-tea-4
```

Yes. We can get our cups of tea off. It we try to take again from the tea-channel, we get a nil. The channel is drained of values. There is no more tea:

```
(async/<!! tea-channel)
;; -> nil
```

nil is special. Note that you cannot put it on a channel:

```
(async/>!! tea-channel nil)
;; IllegalArgumentException Can't put nil on channel
```

nil lets us know that the channel is empty.

Now that we know how to do this synchronously, it would be nice to see how we can do this asynchronously. We can do this within a go block and an async put and take:

- An async put is indicated by >!. It puts data on the channel and needs to be used with a go block.

- An async get is indicated by <!. It gets data off of the channel and needs to be used with a go block.

```
(let [tea-channel (async/chan)]
  (async/go (async/>! tea-channel :cup-of-tea-1))
  (async/go (println "Thanks for the " (async/<! tea-channel))))

;; Will print to stdout:
;; Thanks for the  :cup-of-tea-1
```

It's nice to get a value from a channel asynchronously once, but we can set up a go-loop that will continuously execute, waiting on value from a channel:

```
(def tea-channel (async/chan 10))

(async/go-loop []
              (println "Thanks for the " (async/<! tea-channel))
              (recur))
```

After you evaluate the async/go-loop, the loop will wait in the background automatically listening for anything that is put on the tea-channel. We can put as many values on our channel as we want, and they will automatically be pulled off, the println executed, and then it will wait again for more input. To see it in action try:

```
(async/>!! tea-channel :hot-cup-of-tea)

;; Will print to stdout:
;; Thanks for the  :hot-cup-of-tea

(async/>!! tea-channel :tea-with-sugar)

;; Will print to stdout:
;; Thanks for the  :tea-with-sugar

(async/>!! tea-channel :tea-with-milk)

;; Will print to stdout:
;; Thanks for the  :tea-with-milk
```

What is going on with this go-loop? Everything within the go block has its own special pool of threads. A take from the channel, which would normally block, will only pause the execution instead. The go-loop will act just like a go with a nested loop inside. That is, it will take a value off the channel when it is available, then recur, and wait for the next value, as shown in Figure 6-2.

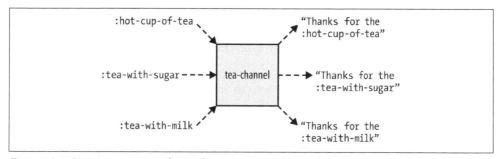

Figure 6-2. Putting tea on a channel

So far, we have only looked at values from one channel. But there is a way with *core.async* that we can look at multiple channels and get the value from the one that arrives first. We can use alts!. To show this in an example, let's have three channels instead of just one. In addition to our tea channel, we can have ones that will deliver milk and sugar:

```
(def tea-channel (async/chan 10))
(def milk-channel (async/chan 10))
(def sugar-channel (async/chan 10))
```

Now let's create our go-loop that will combine input on all these channels with the alts:

```
(async/go-loop []
               (let [[v ch] (async/alts! [tea-channel
                                          milk-channel
                                          sugar-channel])]
                 (println "Got " v " from " ch)
                 (recur)))
```

We can add input to any of the channels and the go-loop will process the input from whatever channel has the value:

```
(async/>!! sugar-channel :sugar)

;; Will print to stdout:
;;Got  :sugar  from  #<ManyToManyChannel@2555e95>

(async/>!! milk-channel :milk)
;; Will print to stdout:
;; Got  :milk  from  ManyToManyChannel@1a1850e5


(async/>!! tea-channel :tea)
;; Will print to stdout:
;; Got  :tea  from  #ManyToManyChannel@130f42ba>
```

The ability to wait for input across many channels, combined with the fact that these go blocks are not bound to threads and are very lightweight processes, makes this a very powerful feature. We could have lots of channels. This can be especially useful when you want to get information or poll endpoints across a network, while not blocking your main processing.

We have been learning and exploring how to work with channels and go blocks. We finally have enough background to create an async tea party for our project.

Serving Tea at a core.async Tea Party

In this tea party example, we are interested in getting our tea fast. We are going to use two tea services, *The Google Tea Service* and *The Yahoo! Tea Service*. When we request our tea, we will ask them both for tea, but return the tea service that comes back the fastest, as shown in Figure 6-3.

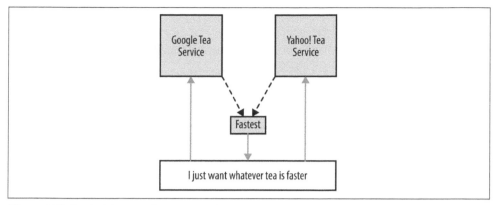

Figure 6-3. Fastest tea service

We are going to have to create two channels, one for Google and one for Yahoo!. Go ahead and edit your *core.clj* file to require the async namespace and define the channels:

```
(ns async-tea-party.core
  (:require [clojure.core.async :as async]))

(def google-tea-service-chan (async/chan 10))
(def yahoo-tea-service-chan (async/chan 10))
```

We don't actually want to call the real Google or real Yahoo!. So far as I know, they don't actually serve tea yet. But we will simulate calling them and having it take a random amount of time. This random amount of time will be a function called `random-add`. It uses a `rand-int` function that picks a random integer between 0 and 100,000. Then it uses it in a function that will sum up a vector filled with the number 1 of a random length:

```
(defn random-add []
  (reduce + (conj [] (repeat (rand-int 100000) 1))))
```

When we request the *Google Tea Service*, we will use a *core.async* go block to randomly sleep. After we are done sleeping, we will put the string "tea compliments of google" on the `google-tea-service-chan`, signaling that the tea is ready:

```
(defn request-google-tea-service []
  (async/go
    (random-add)
    (async/>! google-tea-service-chan
              "tea compliments of google")))
```

We will do the same thing when requesting tea from the *Yahoo! Tea Service*:

```
(defn request-yahoo-tea-service []
  (async/go
    (random-add)
```

```
(async/>! yahoo-tea-service-chan
         "tea compliments of yahoo")))
```

Finally, we will create function to request tea that will call both services and return the fastest one (this, of course, will use our alts!):

```
(defn request-tea []
  (request-google-tea-service)   ❶
  (request-yahoo-tea-service)    ❷
  (async/go (let [[v] (async/alts!  ❸
                       [google-tea-service-chan
                        yahoo-tea-service-chan])]
              (println v))))  ❹
```

❶ Request the Google tea, which will sleep randomly and put the tea string on the google-tea-service-chan.

❷ Request the Yahoo! tea, which will sleep randomly and put the tea string on the yahoo-tea-service-chan.

❸ Listen on both the Google and Yahoo! channel to see what service returns first.

❹ Print out the value from the channel that came first.

At this point, your *core.clj* file should have the following code:

```
(ns async-tea-party.core
  (:require [clojure.core.async :as async]))

(def google-tea-service-chan (async/chan 10))
(def yahoo-tea-service-chan (async/chan 10))

(defn random-add []
  (reduce + (conj [] (repeat 1 (rand-int 100000)))))

(defn request-google-tea-service []
  (async/go
    (random-add)
    (async/>! google-tea-service-chan
              "tea compliments of google")))

(defn request-yahoo-tea-service []
  (async/go
   (random-add)
   (async/>! yahoo-tea-service-chan
             "tea compliments of yahoo")))

(defn request-tea []
  (request-google-tea-service)
  (request-yahoo-tea-service)
  (async/go (let [[v] (async/alts!
```

```
          [google-tea-service-chan
           yahoo-tea-service-chan])]
    (println v))))
```

Let's give it try. Go ahead and call the `request-tea` function. It will print either "tea compliments of yahoo" or "tea compliments of google." This depends, of course, on which returned first:

```
(request-tea)
;; Will print to stdout
;; tea compliments of yahoo
```

Try it a few more times and see if it changes between Yahoo! and Google.

 If you run into any troubles with your example, try restarting your REPL in case you forgot to evaluate something.

Great! We have our async tea party up and running. We can communicate our values asynchronously to other channels and coordinate behavior to each of them. We are going to take this even further by creating some code and running it from the command line.

Creating a Tea Party to Be Run from the Command Line

To be able to request tea from the command line, we are going to have to tweak our program a little bit. One problem we currently have is that we are only printing the result asynchronously from our tea service. If we call the `request-tea` function from the command line, the program does not know to wait for our line to print out. It will most likely exit before we are done.

To fix this, we are going to create another channel for the result of the fastest tea web service. Once we get the result from either Google or Yahoo!, we will put the value on the result channel. This way, we can do a blocking get of the value on the result channel and ensure that we can get our tea before our program exits.

Go ahead and edit the *core.clj* file with the result channel and modifications to the `request-tea` function:

```
(def result-chan (async/chan 10))

(defn request-tea []
  (request-google-tea-service)
  (request-yahoo-tea-service)
  (async/go (let [[v] (async/alts!
                       [google-tea-service-chan
```

```
        yahoo-tea-service-chan])]
    (async/>! result-chan v)))) ❶
```

❶ Here we are putting the fastest tea result on the result-chan.

We need a couple more things before we can run this from the command line. The first thing need is a -main- function to run as a program entry point. In it, we will display a message that it is requesting tea and call the request-tea function. Finally, it will use a blocking get to retrieve the fastest tea service value from result-chan:

```
(defn -main [& args]
  (println "Requesting tea!")
  (request-tea)
  (println (async/<!! result-chan)))
```

We need to add our :gen-class key to the namespace. This will generate a class for it to eventually run as a standalone program. We also need the :main keyword in the project.clj file that will tell it what namespace is the entry point.

So putting it all together, your project.clj should look like this:

```
(defproject async-tea-party "0.1.0-SNAPSHOT"
  :description "FIXME: write description"
  :url "http://example.com/FIXME"
  :license {:name "Eclipse Public License"
            :url "http://www.eclipse.org/legal/epl-v10.html"}
  :dependencies [[org.clojure/clojure "1.6.0"]
                 [org.clojure/core.async "0.1.346.0-17112a-alpha"]]
  :main async-tea-party.core)
```

Your core.clj should look like this:

```
(ns async-tea-party.core
  (:gen-class)
  (:require [clojure.core.async :as async]))

(def google-tea-service-chan (async/chan 10))
(def yahoo-tea-service-chan (async/chan 10))
(def result-chan (async/chan 10))

(defn random-add []
  (reduce + (conj [] (repeat 1 (rand-int 100000)))))

(defn request-google-tea-service []
  (async/go
    (random-add)
    (async/>! google-tea-service-chan
                  "tea compliments of google")))

(defn request-yahoo-tea-service []
  (async/go
    (random-add)
```

```
    (async/>! yahoo-tea-service-chan
                   "tea compliments of yahoo")))

(defn request-tea []
  (request-google-tea-service)
  (request-yahoo-tea-service)
  (async/go (let [[v] (async/alts!
                         [google-tea-service-chan
                          yahoo-tea-service-chan])]
              (async/>! result-chan v))))

(defn -main [& args]
  (println "Requesting tea!")
  (request-tea)
  (println (async/<!! result-chan)))
```

Now you can try to run it! Go to your command prompt in the top level of your project and type in **lein run**.

It should look something like this:

```
-> lein run
Requesting tea!
tea compliments of yahoo
```

Try again and see if you get a different result. Because we are doing a random sleep, the result might be different each time:

```
-> lein run
Requesting tea!
tea compliments of google
```

It would be nice if we could share this with others without them having to run it with Leiningen. We can do this by packaging up our code in an *uberjar*. This is a JAR file that contains everything it needs to run, including Clojure.

Sharing Your Tea Party with Others by Creating an Uberjar

We can create uberjars quite easily with Leiningen. One more thing we need in the *project.clj* file is the :aot keyword. It will enable *ahead-of-time* compilation, which is useful for Clojure code that is run from the command line.

In your *project.clj* file, add the following :aot keyword:

```
(defproject async-tea-party "0.1.0-SNAPSHOT"
  :description "FIXME: write description"
  :url "http://example.com/FIXME"
  :license {:name "Eclipse Public License"
            :url "http://www.eclipse.org/legal/epl-v10.html"}
  :dependencies [[org.clojure/clojure "1.6.0"]
                 [org.clojure/core.async "0.1.346.0-17112a-alpha"]]
```

```
:main async-tea-party.core
:aot [async-tea-party.core])
```

In the top level of your project, type **lein uberjar** at your command prompt.

You should see that two JARs were created in your target directory:

```
Compiling async-tea-party.core
Created target/async-tea-party-0.1.0-SNAPSHOT.jar
Created target/async-tea-party-0.1.0-SNAPSHOT-standalone.jar
```

This first JAR is the regular JAR with your project classes and the *core.async* dependencies. The second standalone JAR is the one that has all the Clojure classes included in it. This is the one that we can actually run with the java -jar command. Type the following at the command line:

```
java -jar ./target/async-tea-party-0.1.0-SNAPSHOT-standalone.jar
```

This is the output you should see:

```
Requesting tea!
tea compliments of yahoo
```

You have just created a Clojure project with asynchronous communication. It can also be run on the command line and shared with your friends.

So far we have been exploring Clojure running on the JVM, but it also runs on the browser with ClojureScript. In fact, the *core.async* library runs with ClojureScript too, bringing asynchronous communication to your browser, all without callbacks!

We'll look into the world of running Clojure on the Web with web servers and ClojureScript in the next chapter.

CHAPTER 7

Creating Web Applications with Clojure

Get ready for some fun. This is where it all comes together. We are going to make a web application with Clojure. At the end of this chapter, you will have a working Clojure web app that is not only Clojure on the web server, but also on the frontend with ClojureScript.

Let's jump in and start. We will begin with getting a web server up and running, which will involve creating a Clojure project with Leiningen, and using a Clojure library called *Compojure*.

Creating a Web Server with Compojure

Compojure is a Clojure library that provides simple routing for an another lower-level web application library called *Ring*. One of nice features of *Ring* is that it allows web applications to be built in modular components. As a result, there is not one particular web app framework that people use in Clojure. Rather, libraries are used, composed, and shared among many applications.

We need a theme. We have been saving one of my favorite encounters in *Alice in Wonderland* for this example, the time when Alice meets the ever delightful, smiling Cheshire Cat. In honor of him, our project will be named *cheshire-cat*. At the end of our example, we will have a Clojure server with a ClojureScript frontend that will make a Cheshire Cat fade away (*https://github.com/gigasquid/cheshire-cat*).

In our example, we are purposely going to focus on routing, JSON, and simple ClojureScript actions so that you can get a good understanding of the basics. Afterward, we will touch on further areas to explore such as templating, databases, and other libraries and frameworks.

To create a new project with Leiningen, we would normally type **lein new cheshire-cat**, then manually add the library dependencies that we need and start creating our code. However, with a new Compojure project, we can use a template, to help us skip some configuration steps. It will automatically create a skeleton web application for us.

Go ahead and open a command prompt and type in **lein new compojure cheshire-cat**.

Type **cd cheshire-cat** to go into the newly created directory and let's see what it made. You should see the following directory structure:

```
├── README.md
├── project.clj
├── resources
│   └── public
├── src
│   └── cheshire_cat
│       └── handler.clj
└── test
    └── cheshire_cat
        └── handler.clj
6 directories, 6 files
```

It looks very similar to our other project structures, with a couple differences. There is a new *resources/public* directory. This is for the web application to use and is the standard place to put images, CSS, and JavaScript files. It also created a source and test file called *handler.clj*.

 Compojure automatically downloads the *latest version* of the template. If the code you see after running the template doesn't match the code in the book, don't panic. You happen to have a more up-to-date copy. To follow along with the example, just replace the contents of your *project.clj* and *handler.clj* files with what you see in the book.

Before diving into the code, let's check out what the generated *README* file has to say:

```
# cheshire-cat

FIXME

## Prerequisites

You will need [Leiningen][] 2.0.0 or above installed.

[leiningen]: https://github.com/technomancy/leiningen
```

```
## Running

To start a web server for the application, run:

    lein ring server

## License

Copyright ¬© 2015 FIXME
```

Great! We can run the web server with the command `lein ring server`. Go ahead and try that from your command line and see what happens:

```
->  lein ring server
2015-01-09 09:10:05.033:INFO:oejs.Server:jetty-7.6.8.v20121106
2015-01-09 09:10:05.080:INFO:oejs.AbstractConnector:Started...
Started server on port 3000
```

A web server was started on port 3000 for us. It also automatically opened a browser, with the text "Hello World" displayed, as shown in Figure 7-1.

Figure 7-1. Hello World Ring server

This is great. We have a minimal web server all set up for us to build on. Before we do, let's step back and take a closer look at the files that the Compojure template Leiningen created for us, so we can get a feel for how it all works.

Let's look at the *src/cheshire_cat/handler.clj* file:

```
(ns cheshire-cat.handler
  (:require [compojure.core :refer :all]
            [compojure.route :as route]
            [ring.middleware.defaults :refer [wrap-defaults site-defaults]]))

(defroutes app-routes ❶
  (GET "/" [] "Hello World") ❷
  (route/not-found "Not Found")) ❸

(def app
  (wrap-defaults app-routes site-defaults)) ❹
```

❶ defroutes is used to create a sequence of HTTP routes called app-routes. These are the request paths that the web application will handle.

❷ GET is used to create an HTTP get route that we saw when we hit the base URL. In this case, it is the "/" path. It returned the string "Hello World".

❸ route/not-found is used to create a basic 404 handler. If someone asks for a path that is not defined, like "/foo", it will return "Not Found" with a 404 status.

❹ Here, we are creating app using the *handler/site* on all of our routes. This sets up some basic middleware needed on standard websites, such as parameter, session, cookie handling, and handling our resource files like images, CSS, and JavaScript. There are many middleware options. For other projects, you might want to check out other standard configurations such as api, and secure site defaults. They can be found in the Ring Defaults library (*https://github.com/ring-clojure/ring-defaults*).

The app handler is the main entry point into our application. Let's next open up the *project.clj* file and see how it all ties together:

```
(defproject cheshire-cat "0.1.0-SNAPSHOT"
  :description "FIXME: write description"
  :url "http://example.com/FIXME"
  :min-lein-version "2.0.0"
  :dependencies [[org.clojure/clojure "1.6.0"]
                 [compojure "1.3.1"]
                 [ring/ring-defaults "0.1.2"]]
  :plugins [[lein-ring "0.8.13"]] ❶
  :ring {:handler cheshire-cat.core.handler/app} ❷
  :profiles
  {:dev {:dependencies [[javax.servlet/servlet-api "2.5"]]}})
```

The important parts here are the keys :plugins and :ring.

❶ The lein-ring plug-in provides automation for common Ring tasks, like starting up the web server.

❷ The :ring :handler key tells the startup web server task where to find the main app routes. Here it points to the app that we had created in the cheshire-cat-handler namespace.

So with our simple Compojure app, we can start up a web server and have it respond to a collection of routes that we define. Let's try to add our own route. Open up and edit the *handler.clj* file to respond to a new route called /cheshire-cat.

Add the following line to your defroutes:

```
(GET "/cheshire-cat" [] "Smile!")

(ns cheshire-cat.core.handler
  (:require [compojure.core :refer :all]
            [compojure.route :as route]
            [ring.middleware.defaults :refer [wrap-defaults site-defaults]]))

(defroutes app-routes
  (GET "/" [] "Hello World")
  (GET "/cheshire-cat" [] "Smile!")
  (route/not-found "Not Found"))

(def app
  (wrap-defaults app-routes site-defaults))
```

In your browser, you can now go to *http://localhost:3000/cheshire-cat*. It should look like Figure 7-2.

Figure 7-2. Ring response in text/HTML

This is fun. But so far we have just been serving up a plain-text/HTML response. To get ready to communicate with the frontend, we are going to want a more flexible JSON response. First, we will need to use a library for creating JSON out of Clojure data structures. It just so happens that a Clojure library that handles JSON transformations is named after our cat. It is called *Cheshire*.

Using JSON with the Cheshire Library and Ring

Cheshire is a library for encoding and decoding JSON. It can be found on GitHub (*https://github.com/dakrone/cheshire*). Let's include Cheshire in our project and use it to return a JSON response from our web server when we hit our cheshire-cat route.

The first thing to do is to include it in our dependency list in our *project.clj* file. Add this line to your *project.clj* file:

```
[cheshire "5.4.0"]

(defproject cheshire-cat "0.1.0-SNAPSHOT"
  :description "FIXME: write description"
  :url "http://example.com/FIXME"
  :min-lein-version "2.0.0"
  :dependencies [[org.clojure/clojure "1.6.0"]
```

```
                [compojure "1.3.1"]
                [ring/ring-defaults "0.1.2"]
                [cheshire "5.4.0"]]
    :plugins [[lein-ring "0.8.13"]]
    :ring {:handler cheshire-cat.core.handler/app}
    :profiles
    {:dev {:dependencies [[javax.servlet/servlet-api "2.5"]
                          [ring-mock "0.1.5"]]}})
```

Because we added a new dependency, we need to restart the web server. Find the terminal where your `lein ring server` is running and restart it.

 You can also start the web server with `lein ring server-headless`. This will start up the web server and not open a new window for you.

Now we are ready to change our handler to return a JSON response. Open up the *handler.clj* file in the editor. First, we need to add the Cheshire library to the namespace so that we can use it. Add it to the `:require` (feel free to use Ctl-C and copy the code):

```
(ns cheshire-cat.core.handler
  (:require [compojure.core :refer :all]
            [compojure.route :as route]
            [ring.middleware.defaults :refer [wrap-defaults site-defaults]]
            [cheshire.core :as json]))
```

Before we move on, let's take a moment to understand the basics of parsing and generating JSON with the Cheshire library. We can do this in the REPL. There are two main functions: `generate-string`, which encodes to JSON, and `parse-string`, which decodes from JSON. Let's take a look at both.

Encoding with `generate-string` takes a Clojure data structure and turns it into a JSON string:

```
(json/generate-string {:name "Cheshire Cat" :state :grinning})
;; -> "{\"name\":\"Cheshire Cat\",\"state\":\"grinning\"}"
```

Decoding with `parse-string` does the reverse: it takes a JSON-encoded string and returns the data structure. By default, it will return map keys as strings:

```
(json/parse-string
 "{\"name\":\"Cheshire Cat\",\"state\":\"grinning\"}")
;; -> {"name" "Cheshire Cat", "state" "grinning"}
```

However, if you supply a true as the second argument, `json/parse-string` will transform the keys in the result to keywords:

```
(json/parse-string
  "{\"name\":\"Cheshire Cat\",\"state\":\"grinning\"}" true)
;; -> {:name "Cheshire Cat", :state "grinning"}
```

Now that we know the basics of how to deal with JSON transformations, let's turn our attention to how we can transform our route into a JSON response.

Ring deals with maps as both the request and response. This means that we just need to specify the HTTP response form that we want to return in the handler function. Edit the app-routes to return a JSON response map for our route:

```
(defroutes app-routes
  (GET "/" [] "Hello World")
  (GET "/cheshire-cat" []
       {:status 200 ❶
        :headers {"Content-Type" "application/json; charset=utf-8"} ❷
        :body (json/generate-string ❸
                {:name "Cheshire Cat"
                 :status :grinning})})
  (route/not-found "Not Found"))
```

❶ We have the HTTP status of the response. Here we want to return a 200 (everything is fine).

❷ The content type for the response is specified. Here is where we say that we want to return a JSON response rather than an HTML/text one.

❸ The body is our data. It, of course, must be in JSON format. Here is where we use the Cheshire library to generate a JSON string out of our Clojure map.

Let's try it out. If you have a Mac or Linux machine, open a terminal and type in the following:

```
curl -i http://localhost:3000/cheshire-cat
```

If you are on Windows, you can go to *http://localhost:3000/cheshire-cat* in Google Chrome or Firefox and it will display the JSON data. The result from the curl will look like this:

```
-> curl -i http://localhost:3000/cheshire-cat
HTTP/1.1 200 OK
Date: Fri, 09 Jan 2015 14:28:40 GMT
X-Content-Type-Options: nosniff
X-Frame-Options: SAMEORIGIN
X-XSS-Protection: 1; mode=block
Set-Cookie: ring-session=75cbd025-9672-43fe-8718-2d357c39dac0;Path=/;HttpOnly
Content-Type: application/json; charset=utf-8
Content-Length: 43
Server: Jetty(7.6.8.v20121106)

{"name":"Cheshire Cat","status":"grinning"}
```

We have a JSON endpoint now.

You may be wondering why we didn't have to specify the whole map response before, when we returned "Smile!". Or indeed, when we hit the *http://localhost:3000/* base URL that returns "Hello World". This is because the Compojure library provides some intelligence for us. If a string is returned as a route response, it will turn it into a standard response like this:

```
{:status 200
 :headers {"Content-Type" "text/html; charset=utf-8"}
 :body "Hello World"}
```

If you are planning on creating an API where all the routes will be JSON, you are most likely not going to manually craft the response on each of them. In this case, we can use Ring middleware to automate this process for us. The Ring-JSON (*https://github.com/ring-clojure/ring-json*) library does just this. It will automatically convert any response with a Clojure collection as a body into JSON for you, and it uses Cheshire to do it.

As an exercise, let's go ahead and use this middleware to create our JSON response. First, of course, we will need to update our *project.clj* file to include the ring-json library. While we are at it, we can remove the Cheshire one, because we won't need to use it directly anymore:

```
(defproject cheshire-cat "0.1.0-SNAPSHOT"
  :description "FIXME: write description"
  :url "http://example.com/FIXME"
  :min-lein-version "2.0.0"
  :dependencies [[org.clojure/clojure "1.6.0"]
                 [compojure "1.3.1"]
                 [ring/ring-defaults "0.1.2"]
                 [ring/ring-json "0.3.1"]]
  :plugins [[lein-ring "0.8.13"]]
  :ring {:handler cheshire-cat.core.handler/app}
  :profiles
  {:dev {:dependencies [[javax.servlet/servlet-api "2.5"]
                        [ring-mock "0.1.5"]]}})
```

You will also need to restart your web server again because we will need to pull down the new library. Go ahead and stop the one that is running and type in **lein ring server** to restart.

We can now turn our attention to editing the *handler.clj* file. You will want to remove cheshire.core from the namespace and add the following lines instead:

```
[ring.middleware.json :as ring-json]
[ring.util.response :as rr]
```

Now, we can remove the handcrafted response in the /cheshire-cat route, and just leave the Clojure data structure and the response:

```
(GET "/cheshire-cat" []
     (rr/response {:name "Cheshire Cat" :status :grinning}))
```

The `ring.util.response/response` function creates a basic, status 200 map for us with a body. If you go ahead and try it in your REPL, you will see:

```
(rr/response {:name "Cheshire Cat" :status :grinning})
;; -> {:status 200,
;;     :headers {},
;;     :body {:name "Cheshire Cat", :status :grinning}
;;     }
```

Finally, we can add the middleware JSON wrapping of the body in our app definition:

```
(def app
  (-> app-routes
    (ring-json/wrap-json-response)
    (wrap-defaults site-defaults)))
```

This is taking our `app-routes` and first wrapping them with the site-defaults and then wrapping it with our automatic JSON response, using the Cheshire library to automatically convert any collection that is in the body of the response to JSON.

Putting it all together, the whole *handler.clj* file is now:

```
(ns cheshire-cat.core.handler
  (:require [compojure.core :refer :all]
            [compojure.route :as route]
            [ring.middleware.defaults :refer [wrap-defaults site-defaults]]
            [ring.middleware.json :as ring-json]
            [ring.util.response :as rr]))

(defroutes app-routes
  (GET "/" [] "Hello World")
  (GET "/cheshire-cat" []
       (rr/response {:name "Cheshire Cat" :status :grinning}))
  (route/not-found "Not Found"))

(def app
  (-> app-routes
      (ring-json/wrap-json-response)
      (wrap-defaults site-defaults)))
```

Let's try out our `cheshire-cat` route with a curl in our terminal. Type in the following:

```
curl -i http://localhost:3000/cheshire-cat
```

If you have a system that supports curl, you will see the following:

```
HTTP/1.1 200 OK
Date: Wed, 22 Oct 2014 13:22:01 GMT
Content-Type: application/json; charset=utf-8
Content-Length: 43
```

```
Server: Jetty(7.6.8.v20121106)
```

```
{"name":"Cheshire Cat","status":"grinning"}
```

You have just created a web server that can handle both HTML and JSON responses. We are now at a point where we can communicate with the browser by having Java-Script hit the endpoint, get the data from the response, and do something interesting with it. Does this mean leaving Clojure behind? Not at all. With ClojureScript, we can use Clojure in the browser as well as on the server.

Using Clojure in Your Browser with ClojureScript

ClojureScript is a subset of the Clojure language that compiles down to JavaScript. It uses Google's Closure compiler (*https://github.com/google/closure-compiler*) (the name unfortunately sounds the same as Clojure and causes some confusion, but is totally different) behind the scenes to do this. Using Google's Closure compiler has two main advantages. ClojureScript has access to a full breadth of Google Closure libraries. In addition to all the Closure libraries, it can also use a JavaScript library, like JQuery and React. The other main advantage is the Closure compiler is really smart. It has different compilation modes and in the advanced modes it does some pretty amazing code optimizations, like dead code analysis.

How do we get started with ClojureScript? It is just a library, so we add it to our *project.clj* file and have Leiningen get it for us. To follow along with this demo, add the following version to your cheshire-cat *project.clj* file:

```
[org.clojure/clojurescript "0.0-2371"]
```

We are also going to use a Leiningen plug-in to help make working with Clojure-Script a bit easier. The lein-cljsbuild (*https://github.com/emezeske/lein-cljsbuild*) plug-in allows you to autocompile your ClojureScript code while you are working on it, and it also provides a nice ClojureScript REPL as well. Go ahead and add a dependency for this as well in your :plugins section:

```
:plugins [[lein-ring "0.8.13"]
          [lein-cljsbuild "1.0.3"]]
```

With cljsbuild, we also need to specify some other configuration for our project. In your *project.clj* file, add a key for :cljsbuild and add the following:

```
:cljsbuild {
    :builds [{
        :source-paths ["src-cljs"]    ❶
        :compiler {
          :output-to "resources/public/main.js"  ❷
          :optimizations :whitespace   ❸
          :pretty-print true}}]}        ❹
```

❶ This tells `cljsbuild` where to look for our ClojureScript code. It will look for it in a directory named *src-cljs* (we still need to create that).

❷ It will compile our ClojureScript code and write it all to a JavaScript file named *main.js* in our *resources* directory.

❸ The optimization level of the Google Closure compiler will be *whitespace*, which means that it will remove extra whitespace. This is a good level for development, because you can look at the output and debug the code easily. For production code, you can set it to an advanced level.

❹ `:pretty-print` makes the output more human readable—always a good thing in development.

You whole *project.clj* file should now look like this:

```
(defproject cheshire-cat "0.1.0-SNAPSHOT"
  :description "FIXME: write description"
  :url "http://example.com/FIXME"
  :min-lein-version "2.0.0"
  :dependencies [[org.clojure/clojure "1.6.0"]
                 [compojure "1.3.1"]
                 [ring/ring-defaults "0.1.2"]
                 [ring/ring-json "0.3.1"]
                 [org.clojure/clojurescript "0.0-2371"]]
  :plugins [[lein-ring "0.8.13"]
            [lein-cljsbuild "1.0.3"]]
  :ring {:handler cheshire-cat.core.handler/app}
  :profiles
  {:dev {:dependencies [[javax.servlet/servlet-api "2.5"]
                        [ring-mock "0.1.5"]]}}
  :cljsbuild {
    :builds [{
        :source-paths ["src-cljs"]
        :compiler {
          :output-to "resources/public/main.js"
          :optimizations :whitespace
          :pretty-print true}}]})
```

Let's try it out by getting a ClojureScript REPL up and running.

Get a terminal open in the root of the project and type in the following:

```
lein trampoline cljsbuild repl-rhino
```

This will use Rhino JavaScript to evaluate the end result from the ClojureScript that you enter as input. It is the simplest ClojureScript REPL to get up and running.

You will see a ClojureScript REPL waiting for you:

```
-> lein trampoline cljsbuild repl-rhino
Running Rhino-based ClojureScript REPL.
To quit, type: :cljs/quit
ClojureScript:cljs.user>
```

Try something easy, like adding two numbers:

```
ClojureScript:cljs.user> (+ 1 1)
;; => 2
```

It looks just like our regular Clojure REPL, but things are really quite a bit different. Let's see what happens when we try to look at the class of a string:

```
(class "hi")
;; -> "Error evaluating:" (class "hi") ...
;;      TypeError: Cannot call method "call" of undefined
```

We are no longer on the JVM. There are no classes here in JavaScript. But we can do different things. We can do interop with JavaScript functions by using a `js/` prefix. For example, we can look at the JavaScript `Date` function:

```
js/Date
;; -> #<function Date() { [native code for Date.Date, arity=1] }
```

We can also execute the `Date` function by calling it in parens:

```
(js/Date)
;; ->"Sun Oct 26 2014 11:27:20 GMT-0400 (EDT)"
```

Collections and their functions all work the same as in Clojure:

```
(first [1 2 3 4])
;; ->1
```

However, concurrency using agents and refs are not available. But we do have atoms:

```
(def x (atom 0))
;; -> #<Atom: 0>

(swap! x inc)
;; -> 1
```

It is good to remember that there are differences between Clojure and ClojureScript although they do share core language structures and features. These are the major differences to take note of:

- ClojureScript has JavaScript interop rather than Java.
- Although there are atoms, there are no agents or refs.
- In ClojureScript, only integer and floating-point numbers are supported.
- Of course, ClojureScript compiles to JavaScript.

ClojureScript looks very similar to Clojure, but there are some differences.

So far, we have just been experimenting in the REPL with plain ClojureScript. But we want to be able to interact with the browser and use HTML with it. For that we need to do a bit more setup. We will need a ClojureScript file, and of course, an HTML page to display and call it.

In our *project.clj* :cljsbuild configuration, we specified that our ClojureScript files would live in the *src-cljs* directory of the root of our project. So, we will need to create that directory using mkdir or your operating system's equivalent method.

Then, go ahead a create a ClojureScript file named *core.cljs* with the following:

```
(ns cheshire-cat.core)

(defn ^:export init [] ❶
  (js/alert "hi")) ❷
```

❶ This is the main entry point to our ClojureScript from the browser. We are using the ^:export metadata on this function, so that it will be exposed as a function that JavaScript can call from the global context. Why do we have to do this? Because the Google Closure compiler can be very aggressive about the size of the files it generates. It might even change the function names and make them shorter. However, with the *whitespace* optimization defined in our *project.clj* file, it is not really needed.

❷ We are calling the JavaScript alert function to display "hi" for us when we load the page.

 Clojure *metadata* like ^:export allows you to annotate functions and pass additional information to the compiler.

Create a *cat.html* file in the *resources/public* directory with the following contents:

```
<!DOCTYPE html>
<html>
  <head>
    <title>Cheshire Cat</title>
  </head>
  <body>
    <div id="cat-name">Name</div> ❶
```

```
    <div id="status">Status</div>  ❶

    <script type="text/javascript" src="main.js"></script>  ❷
    <script type="text/javascript">cheshire_cat.core.init()</script>  ❸
  </body>
</html>
```

❶   This is just static text right now. But soon, we will change that with ClojureScript.

❷   The JavaScript file that the browser will load. ClojureScript code will be compiled by `cljsbuild` into this *main.js* file.

❸   This is the main entry point to our ClojureScript namespace. Note that the function is underscored rather than dashed. When the file is compiled, the function is exported with underscores rather than dashes for the namespace, and there is no "/" to separate the namespace from the function.

Get it up and running. We will need two pieces running: the Ring web server to serve up our HTML page, and also the `:cljsbuild` process to compile our ClojureScript to the JavaScript *main.js* file.

To start up the web server (if you don't already have it running), run the following:

```
lein ring server
```

In another terminal run the following:

```
lein cljsbuild auto
```

This command will start a process that will compile your *core.cljs* file to JavaScript. It will continuously monitor the file for changes, and recompile when it detects a change.

You should see that your *core.cljs* file compiled in your `:cljsbuild` terminal:

```
lein cljsbuild auto
Compiling ClojureScript.
Compiling "resources/public/main.js" from ["src-cljs"]...
Successfully compiled "resources/public/main.js" in 6.452 seconds.
```

In your browser, go to *http://localhost:3000/cat.html*. It should look like Figure 7-3.

You have made your first ClojureScript web page!

To see the automatic recompilation the `:cljsbuild` is doing for you, go ahead and edit something small in your *core.cljs* file. For example, change the alert message:

```
(ns cheshire-cat.core)

(defn ^:export init []
  (js/alert "This is fun!"))
```

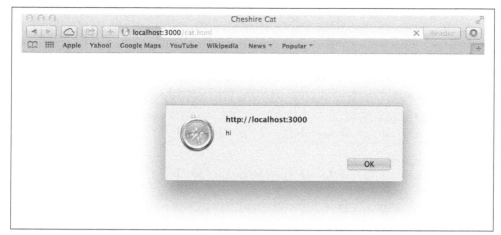

Figure 7-3. ClojureScript web page

When you save the file, the terminal window will show that it is recompiling your file:

```
Successfully compiled "resources/public/main.js" in 0.284 seconds.
Compiling "resources/public/main.js" from ["src-cljs"]...
Successfully compiled "resources/public/main.js" in 0.251 seconds.
```

You can now refresh the *cat.html* page in your browser and see the new alert message.

Let's take a moment to review what you have done. You have added ClojureScript and `lein-cljsbuild` to your project and configured it to compile your ClojureScript when you make changes. You have launched a ClojureScript REPL to experiment with code. Finally, you have created a ClojureScript file and called it from an HTML page.

So far we have been experimenting with ClojureScript in a stand-alone REPL. But we can do more. We can attach this REPL to the browser and be able to make the changes in the REPL happen on the frontend. Using the same basic tools as before we will be able to enter code into our REPL and have a web page magically update in front of our eyes. This is quite exciting for experimentation and rapid feedback when working with the frontend.

Browser-Connected REPL

To do this, there is another `cljsbuild` REPL to use when we want to attach our browser to it. Go ahead and quit your current ClojureScript REPL and restart it as follows:

```
lein trampoline cljsbuild repl-listen
```

This will start up a ClojureScript REPL that is listening on port 9000:

```
-> lein trampoline cljsbuild repl-listen
Running ClojureScript REPL, listening on port 9000.
To quit, type: :cljs/quit
ClojureScript:cljs.user>
```

Now we need to connect to it in our ClojureScript code. We can do this with a couple code changes in our *core.cljs* file. Open up the file and make the following changes:

```
(ns cheshire-cat.core
  (:require [clojure.browser.repl :as repl])) ❶

(defn ^:export init []
  (repl/connect "http://localhost:9000/repl")) ❷
```

❶ We are using the `clojure.browser.repl` namespace so that we can use the REPL connection feature.

❷ The code will connect the browser to the REPL so that any side effects (like alerts showing) will show up in our browser.

You will need to refresh the web page in the browser to execute code and connect the browser to the REPL. Open *http://localhost:3000/cat.html* in the browser.

Finally, you can type in your ClojureScript REPL:

```
(js/alert "This is a browser connected REPL")
```

It will show up in your browser as shown in Figure 7-4.

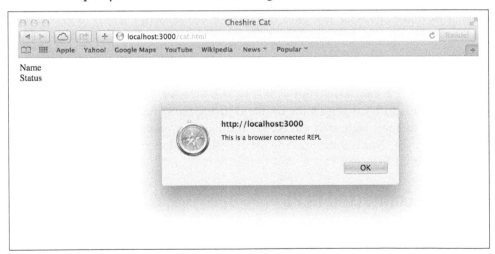

Figure 7-4. ClojureScript with browser-connected REPL

If your alert is not showing up in the browser, refresh your web page.

You can now evaluate code, manipulate the DOM, and interact with your browser application—all from the power of your ClojureScript REPL.

Our project so far has a web server with a /cheshire-cat/ route that we can hit for a JSON response. It also has a ClojureScript-enabled web page. What we want to do is have our ClojureScript be able to hit the JSON endpoint and get the information from the response. For that, we'll need the ClojureScript HTTP library *cljs-http*.

Making HTTP Calls with ClojureScript and cljs-http

The *cljs-http* library is a great way to handle HTTP in ClojureScript. What makes it even more interesting is that it uses the power of *core.async* to handle these calls asynchronously. Let's go ahead and take a closer look at it in action, by calling our cheshire-cat endpoint from our ClojureScript.

In our *project.clj* file, we will need to add the dependencies for the *cljs-http* and *core.async* libraries:

```
:dependencies [[org.clojure/clojure "1.6.0"]
               [compojure "1.3.1"]
               [ring/ring-defaults "0.1.2"]
               [ring/ring-json "0.3.1"]
               [org.clojure/clojurescript "0.0-2371"]
               [cljs-http "0.1.18"]
               [org.clojure/core.async "0.1.346.0-17112a-alpha"]]
```

Because we are downloading some new libraries, we will need to restart our cljsbuild and type in **lein cljsbuild auto**.

Edit your *core.cljs* file to add the following code:

```
(ns cheshire-cat.core
  (:require-macros [cljs.core.async.macros :refer [go]])  ❶
  (:require [clojure.browser.repl :as repl]
            [cljs-http.client :as http]  ❷
            [cljs.core.async :refer [<!]]))  ❸


(defn ^:export init []
  (repl/connect "http://localhost:9000/repl")
  (go  ❹
    (let [response (<! (http/get "/cheshire-cat"))]  ❺
      (js/alert (:body response)))))  ❻
```

❶ This is one of the differences from Clojure. ClojureScript's macros are written in Clojure, rather than ClojureScript, so they are referenced by a special `:require-macros` keyword. Here we are going to be using go. We need this to do HTTP calls in ClojureScript because they use `core.async`.

❷ We will be using the `cljs-http.client` functions and referring to the namespace as *http*.

❸ We will also be needing the asynchronous take (<!) from ClojureScript's *core.async* library.

❹ The code is contained in a go block because the http/get returns a *core.async* channel and we are using the asynchronous take to get the result.

❺ Here we are hitting our `cheshire-cat` endpoint and getting the response from our call asynchronously with a *core.async* take.

❻ Finally, we are showing the body of the response in an alert on the web page.

Refresh the web page after you save your changes and you should see something similar to Figure 7-5.

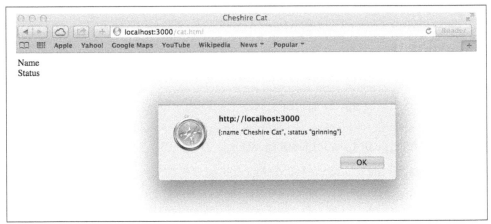

Figure 7-5. ClojureScript with JSON response from server

We are getting data from our endpoint. Now, we need to make changes in the DOM based on the data. For this, we are going to introduce a DOM manipulation and templating library called *Enfocus*.

DOM Control with ClojureScript and Enfocus

To use the Enfocus (*https://github.com/ckirkendall/enfocus*) library, we will need to add it to our dependencies. Add it to your *project.clj* file:

```
:dependencies [[org.clojure/clojure "1.6.0"]
               [compojure "1.3.1"]
               [ring/ring-defaults "0.1.2"]
               [ring/ring-json "0.3.1"]
               [org.clojure/clojurescript "0.0-2371"]
               [cljs-http "0.1.18"]
               [org.clojure/core.async "0.1.346.0-17112a-alpha"]
               [enfocus "2.1.0"]]
```

Also remember to restart your `cljsbuild`.

The Enfocus library works with transformations on the DOM. For example, given a DOM element, we can transform it by setting the content. In our project, we had just gotten back data from our HTTP endpoint call and we want to use it to set the content on the node elements in our *cat.html* file. In particular, we want to:

- Set the div with the id "cat-name" to the data key "name" coming back in our response.

- Set the div with the id "status" to the data key "status" coming back in our response.

We can do this with the Enfocus library. Transformations are handled in an elegant way using the `at` function. You specify *where* you want the transformation to take place in the DOM by giving the `at` function string with a CSS selector. Once you specify where you want the transformation to take place, you need to specify what you actually want done at the node. In our case, we want to set the content of the node, so we can use the `content` function. This code would select the DOM element with id `"cat-name"` and set the text to `"cheshire-cat"`:

```
(at "#cat-name" (content "cheshire-cat"))
```

Open up your *core.cljs* file and add the Enfocus code:

```
(ns cheshire-cat.core
  (:require-macros [cljs.core.async.macros :refer [go]])
  (:require [clojure.browser.repl :as repl]
            [cljs-http.client :as http]
            [cljs.core.async :refer [<!]]
            [enfocus.core :as ef]))  ❶


(defn ^:export init []
  (repl/connect "http://localhost:9000/repl")
```

```
(go (let [response (<! (http/get "/cheshire-cat"))
          body (:body response)] ❷
     (ef/at "#cat-name" (ef/content (:name body))) ❸
     (ef/at "#status" (ef/content (:status body)))))) ❹
```

❶ We require the Enfocus core library and refer to it as ef.

❷ Get the body of the response.

❸ After getting the body of the response, we set the "cat-name" DOM element to
    the content of the :name key in the body.

❹ We also set the "status" DOM element to the content of the :status key in the
    body.

Save your edits, and your cljsbuild will recompile your ClojureScript. After refresh-
ing the *cat.html* page, you should see the screen shown in Figure 7-6.

Figure 7-6. ClojureScript using Enfocus

The Enfocus at function can also handle multiple selectors with transformations, so
we could combine the cat-name and status content updates together:

```
(ef/at "#cat-name" (ef/content (:name body))
       "#status" (ef/content (:status body)))
```

What if we would like to have two transformations at one of the selectors? For example, once we set the content of the status element, we would also like to make the text
really big. First, we need the function to set a style on a node/element. There is a nice
set-style function for this. This will set the font size of a given node to 500% of the
normal text size:

```
(ef/set-style :font-size "500%")
```

Next, to combine the two transformations at the status node, we would use the Enfocus do→ function:

```
(ef/at "#cat-name" (ef/content (:name body))
       "#status" (ef/do->
                    (ef/content (:status body))
                    (ef/set-style :font-size "500%")))
```

Go ahead and edit your *core.cljs* file to include the setting for font-size on the status:

```
(ns cheshire-cat.core
  (:require-macros [cljs.core.async.macros :refer [go]])
  (:require [clojure.browser.repl :as repl]
            [cljs-http.client :as http]
            [cljs.core.async :refer [<!]]
            [enfocus.core :as ef]))


(defn ^:export init []
  (repl/connect "http://localhost:9000/repl")

  (go (let [response (<! (http/get "/cheshire-cat"))
            body  (:body response)]
        (ef/at "#cat-name" (ef/content (:name body))
               "#status" (ef/do->
                           (ef/content (:status body))
                           (ef/set-style :font-size "500%"))))))
```

Refresh your browser and you will see the word "grinning" in large text as shown in Figure 7-7.

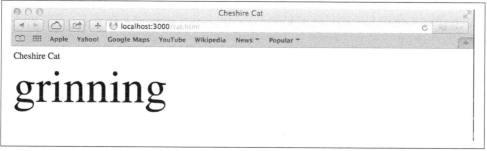

Figure 7-7. ClojureScript with Enfocus transformations

We have explored how to handle DOM transformations with the Enfocus library, but what about event handling? How can we interact with our web page—for example, if we want to execute some ClojureScript when a button is clicked? Luckily, the Enfocus library handles this for us. We will learn about using it next.

Event Handling with Enfocus

Enfocus provides event handling functions in a separate events namespace. Here, we can find a listen function that can listen on an event type and then execute a function when it occurs:

```
(listen :click (fn [event] ))
```

Try this out by adding a button to your HTML page and having something happen when you click it.

First, add a button to your *cat.html* file:

```
<!DOCTYPE html>
<html>
  <head>
    <title>Cheshire Cat</title>
  </head>
  <body>
    <div id="cat-name">Name</div>
    <div id="status">Status</div>
    <button id="button1">Goodbye</button>   ❶

    <script type="text/javascript" src="main.js"></script>
    <script type="text/javascript">cheshire_cat.core.init()</script>
  </body>
</html>
```

❶   Add a button with the id "button1"

Next, we need to edit the ClojureScript code in *core.cljs* to listen for the click event and show an alert. Luckily, the listen function is just another type of transformation on a node, so we can just add it with a selector to our at function:

```
(ns cheshire-cat.core
  (:require-macros [cljs.core.async.macros :refer [go]])
  (:require [clojure.browser.repl :as repl]
            [cljs-http.client :as http]
            [cljs.core.async :refer [<!]]
            [enfocus.core :as ef]
            [enfocus.events :as ev]))   ❶


(defn ^:export init []
  (repl/connect "http://localhost:9000/repl")

  (go (let [response (<! (http/get "/cheshire-cat"))
            body (:body response)]
        (ef/at "#cat-name" (ef/content (:name body))
               "#status" (ef/do->
                            (ef/content (:status body))
                            (ef/set-style :font-size "500%")))
            (ef/at "#button1" (ev/listen   ❷
                                :click   ❸
                                #(js/alert "bye!"))))))   ❹
```

❶   We add the events namespace for Enfocus.

❷   At the button node with the id "button1" we set up a listen event.

❸ We are listening to click events.

❹ When the button is clicked, a function is called to show an alert with the text "bye!".

Save your file and refresh your web page. When you click the Goodbye button, you should see the alert shown in Figure 7-8.

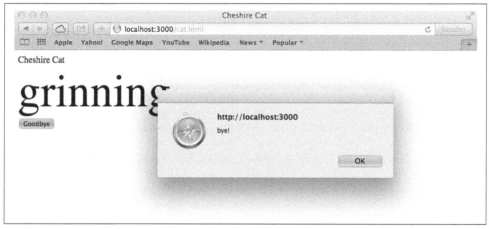

Figure 7-8. ClojureScript with Enfocus event handling

Just one more thing. Enfocus can also do cool stuff like animations. Because we are dealing with the Cheshire Cat, when we click the button to say goodbye, we can fade everything out. But, of course, the grinning text will fade out more slowly than everything else.

We can use the `fade-out` function in the `effects` namespace for the animation. It takes an integer argument of how long the animation will take:

```
(fade-out 500)
```

Add a `say-goodbye` function to your *core.cljs* file that will be called when you click the Goodbye button. It will fade out the cat-name and button at the same rate, but then take a longer while for the grinning status text:

```
(ns cheshire-cat.core
  (:require-macros [cljs.core.async.macros :refer [go]])
  (:require [clojure.browser.repl :as repl]
            [cljs-http.client :as http]
            [cljs.core.async :refer [<!]]
            [enfocus.core :as ef]
            [enfocus.events :as ev]
            [enfocus.effects :as ee])) ❶

(defn say-goodbye [] ❷
```

```
(ef/at
  "#cat-name" (ee/fade-out 500)  ❸
  "#button1" (ee/fade-out 500)   ❸
  "#status" (ee/fade-out 5000)))  ❹

(defn ^:export init []
  (repl/connect "http://localhost:9000/repl")

  (go (let [response (<! (http/get "/cheshire-cat"))
            body (:body response)]
       (ef/at "#cat-name" (ef/content (:name body))
              "#status" (ef/do->
                           (ef/content (:status body))
                           (ef/set-style :font-size "500%")))
       (ef/at "#button1" (ev/listen :click
                                    say-goodbye)))))) ❺
```

❶ Include the enfocus `effects` namespace and alias it to `ee`.

❷ Create a function named `say-goodbye` that will have our animations.

❸ Fade out the name and button nodes over a time of 500ms.

❹ Fade out the status node over a time of 5000ms.

❺ Finally, call our `say-goodbye` function when the button is clicked.

Save the file, refresh your page, and say goodbye to the Cheshire Cat. You should see the name and button disappear quickly, while the grinning text fades slowly. It will look like Figure 7-9.

Figure 7-9. ClojureScript with Enfocus fading effects

You have made a Clojure web application with ClojureScript!

We went through quite a few steps to build our cool web app. Let's take a moment to review.

Summary of Our Clojure and ClojureScript Web Application

We have covered quite a bit in this chapter, starting with web servers and going all the way to ClojureScript and handling DOM transformations and events. Here is a high-level summary of everything we did:

- First, we started with the web server. We created one with Compojure using a Leiningen Clojure template.
- Then, we added "cheshire-cat" route that returned simple HTML/text.
- We learned how to use the *Cheshire* JSON encoding library in Clojure, and had our endpoint return a JSON response.
- Next, we used the Ring Middleware JSON library, *ring-json*, to have our project automatically convert our endpoint to JSON.
- We then added a ClojureScript frontend to our application and learned how to configure our project to use *cljsbuild*.
- We explored the ClojureScript REPL and ClojureScript browser-connected REPL.
- Then, we used `cljs-http` to get the data from our "cheshire-cat" endpoint in ClojureScript.
- Finally, we harnessed the power of the Enfocus library to update the web page with our data, listen for when we clicked the *Goodbye* button, and show an animation to have our grinning Cheshire Cat fade away.

In the Cheshire Cat example, you got a firm foundation in the basics of web servers and routing with Compojure and ClojureScript, and DOM manipulation with the Enfocus library. Next, we are going to discuss some other libraries that you might find useful in developing web applications.

Other Useful Web Development Libraries

The first couple of libraries are ways to do server-side *templating*. That is, creating the HTML structure that will display the web page on the server. The first library to do this is called *Hiccup*.

Using Hiccup for Templating

Hiccup (*https://github.com/weavejester/hiccup*) uses vectors with keywords to generate HTML structure. Here is an example Hiccup form:

```
(use 'hiccup.core)

(html ❶
  [:h1 "Hi there"]  ❷
  [:div.blue "blue div"   ❸
   [:div.yellow "yellow div"  ❹
    [:div#bob "id bob"]]])  ❺
;; -> "<h1>Hi there</h1>
;;       <div class=\"blue\">blue div
;;         <div class=\"yellow\">yellow div
;;           <div id=\"bob\">id bob</div>
;;         </div>
;;       </div>"
```

❶ html is the hiccup function that takes the vector structure and turns it into the HTML markup string.

❷ The beginning of the vector structure is a heading level 1 tag. It is represented by :h1 and has the text "Hi There".

❸ A div is represented by a vector with the keyword :div. It can be given a class with notation of a dot followed by the class name. In this case, it has the class "blue". It contains the text "blue div".

❹ We can nest a div inside another div, by nesting the vector structure. This div has a class "yellow" and contains the text "yellow div".

❺ The final nested div has an id associated with it. The id is "bob" and is represented by the pound sign (#) right after the div.

Hiccup is a simple way to generate HTML on the server side. There is also another way to do this with a library called *Enlive*.

Using Enlive for Templating from Static HTML Files

Enlive (*https://github.com/cgrand/enlive*) also does server-side generating of HTML, but it takes a different approach. It uses static HTML files as templates. It then takes these templates and applies transformations on them. This is very similar to the Enfocus library. In fact, Enlive has an at form transformation that looks very similiar to Enfocus. This is because Enfocus was inspired by the Enlive library. Let's take a quick look at an example.

Once we require the Enlive library, we can define a *snippet*:

```
(require '[net.cgrand.enlive-html :as enlive])

(def my-snippet (enlive/html-snippet
  "<div id='foo'><p>Buttered Scones</p></div>"))
```

Now that we have our snippet, we can do transformations on it using the `at` form. Here we are taking the snippet and selecting the div with the id of "foo". Then we are applying a transformation to set the content of it to the text "Marmalade":

```
(enlive/at my-snippet [:div#foo] (enlive/html-content "Marmalade"))
```

These snippets can be defined in external files rather than in code like we have done in these examples. That way, designers can create and edit them more easily. Finally, these snippets can be combined in logical groupings to form templates. The result is a templating system that is flexible and scales well for bigger web application projects.

Another library to talk about is one that helps with the web server and routing. The name of this library is *Liberator*.

Using Liberator for Content Negotiation and Other Good Things

Liberator (*https://github.com/clojure-liberator/liberator/*) is a very useful library that fits nicely with Ring. One of the really useful things it allows you to do is content negotiation. This is important when your web server needs to support multiple media types such as JSON, plain text, or HTML.

Liberator checks the media type in the `Accept` request header and makes decisions based on it. A quick example of Liberator content negotiation looks like this in a Ring route for `/cat`:

```
(ANY "/cat" []
     (resource :available-media-types ["text/plain"  ❶
                                        "text/html"
                                        "application/json" ]
               :handle-ok  ❷
               #(let [media-type
                      (get-in % [:representation :media-type])]  ❸
                  (case media-type  ❹
                    "text/plain" "Cat"  ❺
                    "text/html" "<html><h2>Cat</h2></html>"  ❻
                    "application/json" {:cat true}))  ❼
               :handle-not-acceptable "No Cats Here!"))  ❽
```

❶ The Liberator `resource` is used to define the available media types for this route. In this case, our `/cat` route will accept `text/plain`, `text/html`, and `application/json`.

❷ We define our resource handler function for a status 200.

❸ The media type from the accept headers are stored in the `:representation` and `:media_type` keys of the request. We bind this to `media-type`.

❹ We then use `media-type` to choose what format of response to return.

❺ Our text/plain response.

❻ Our text/html response.

❼ Our application/json response.

❽ If the request headers do not match with the available media types, the response is handled here.

If the cat route is called, we see the different responses.

If no Accept header is specified, then it means the request would accept any type. Liberator will return the first available media type, which for us is text/plain:

```
-> curl -i   http://localhost:3000/cat
HTTP/1.1 200 OK
Date: Tue, 23 Dec 2014 14:37:40 GMT
Vary: Accept
Content-Type: text/plain;charset=UTF-8
Content-Length: 3
Server: Jetty(7.6.8.v20121106)

Cat
```

If we do specify the Accept header, it will only return the type we ask for. Let's ask for json:

```
-> curl -i -H "Accept: application/json" http://localhost:3000/cat
HTTP/1.1 200 OK
Date: Tue, 23 Dec 2014 14:40:31 GMT
Vary: Accept
Content-Type: application/json;charset=UTF-8
Content-Length: 12
Server: Jetty(7.6.8.v20121106)

{"cat":true}
```

That seems to work fine. One more thing, let's try something that is not an available media type, like application/foo:

```
-> curl -i -H "Accept: application/foo" http://localhost:3000/cat
HTTP/1.1 406 Not Acceptable
Date: Tue, 23 Dec 2014 14:41:40 GMT
Content-Type: text/plain;charset=UTF-8
Content-Length: 13
Server: Jetty(7.6.8.v20121106)

No Cats Here!
```

We get our handle-not-acceptable response.

Liberator can also do other cool things like conditional requests based on the last modified time and etags. The library is well worth checking out for web applications.

We are familiar with JSON as a format for transmitting data from the server to the client, but there is another format released by Rich Hickey and Cognitect called *Transit*.

Using Transit for a Small, Fast JSON Alternative

Transit (*https://github.com/cognitect/transit-clj*) is a set of libraries and a format for sending data between applications. The advantage that it has over JSON is that it has an integrated cache code system that makes it very small and fast. It ships with some standard core types, but it is also extensible.

It is straightforward to use Transit. To encode some data in Transit, you need to specify a byte array output stream and a *transit* writer:

```
(require '[cognitect.transit :as transit])
(import [java.io ByteArrayInputStream ByteArrayOutputStream])

(def out (ByteArrayOutputStream. 4096))
(def writer (transit/writer out :json))
```

Now we can simply write data to it:

```
(transit/write writer "cat")
```

What does the *transit* format look like? We can take a peek by looking at the string representation of the out stream:

```
(.toString out)
;; -> "[\"~#'\",\"cat\"]"
```

The process to read the data from a *transit* input stream is similar. We need an input stream and a *transit* reader:

```
(def in (ByteArrayInputStream. (.toByteArray out)))
(def reader (transit/reader in :json))
```

Then we simply read in the data:

```
(transit/read reader)
;; -> "cat"
```

Transit works in ClojureScript as well with transit-cljs (*https://github.com/cognitect/transit-cljs*), so it is a very nice, fast format to use with Clojure web applications.

Turning our attention to the ClojureScript side of things, we need to mention a very popular and powerful library for creating ClojureScript applications, called *Om*.

Using Om for Powerful Client-Side Applications

Om (*https://github.com/swannodette/om*) is the ClojureScript interface for Facebook's React (*http://facebook.github.io/react/*). It is a very powerful library for building frontend applications. It uses *components* to create applications. One of its advantages is the *reactive* nature of it—if you change a piece of data in the main application state and it is bound to a component, the change will automatically update.

There is a bit of a learning curve to get going on an Om application if you are not familiar with React. Luckily, there are some really good tutorials out there to get you started. Try this Basic Om Tutorial (*https://github.com/swannodette/om/wiki/Basic-Tutorial*) by David Nolen.

So far, we have been talking about libraries that operate on specific areas of a web application like templating, routing, transmission formats, and frontend applications. A couple other libraries that aim to be an inclusive way to build web applications are well worth a look. Their names are *Hoplon* and *Luminus*.

Using Hoplon and Luminus for Inclusive, Bundled Libraries for Web Development

Hoplon (*http://hoplon.io/*) bundles a number of libraries for the aim of a simpler way of creating web applications. The interesting thing about Hoplon is that it comes with a Hoplon compiler. This compiler takes a page written in ClojureScript syntax and then processes it. The output is both HTML and JavaScript. It also uses a build tool named *boot* instead of Leiningen. There is a bit of a learning curve with this way of building web applications as well, but there is very nice documentation (*http://hoplon.io/#/getting-started/*) to get you going.

Luminus (*http://www.luminusweb.net/*) is another set of libraries, or a micro framework, for building web applications. It is built on top of the familiar *Ring* and *Compojure* libraries. It aims to tie these libraries together in a way that makes a simple and rapid development environment. There is a project template (*https://github.com/yogthos/luminus-template*) that provides some sensible defaults to get your web application up and running fast. It also has a very nice documentation site (*http://www.luminusweb.net/docs*).

We have talked about many libraries and micro frameworks, but we haven't really mentioned databases yet. While it is true that they are a crucial part of web development, in Clojure, that database layer is really no big deal.

Dealing with Databases

Clojure web applications don't do anything special with databases. The usual thing to do in a Ring application is just create routes to read and write from the database and create a function to do it. There are many libraries to choose from depending on what database you use and what kind of abstraction you need. Just to name a few, there is java.jdbc (*https://github.com/clojure/java.jdbc*), which is a low-level wrapper for JDBC; and Korma (*http://sqlkorma.com/*), which is an abstraction for SQL queries. Another SQL library is Yesql (*https://github.com/krisajenkins/yesql*), which allows you to keep your SQL queries completely decoupled. If you want a library with the database access already baked in, you can give Luminus a try.

A special note would be to look at Datomic (*http://www.datomic.com/*), which is an immutable database from Rich Hickey that has a rich query capability as well as the special power of looking at the database from a specific point in time.

As you can see, the area of Clojure web development is rich and varied. Now that you know the basics, you might want to explore an area that interests you.

Throughout the book, you have been getting more and more comfortable with Clojure and its ecosystem. We have been saving one of the most powerful features of Clojure for last. The power of macros.

CHAPTER 8

The Power of Macros

You are growing strong with Clojure. Now that you are comfortable, we are returning to the language itself to take a look at an advanced language feature called *macros*. The name might be strange, but it is based on simplicity. Harnessing this simplicity gives it great power.

In fact, you already learned the secret back in Chapter 1—*code is data!* It is contained in the simple sentence.

With this knowledge at the forefront of our minds, let's step forward and explore Clojure macros.

Exploring Macros

Macros are powerful. Macros are awesome. What exactly are they? In practical terms, they are a way to do *meta-programming* in Clojure.

Meta-programming comes from ability of languages to treat their programs as data. This allows a program to modify another program, or *even its own program.*

What can you do with this special ability? In practical terms, macros give you several advantages. They enable you to:

- Create and implement your own language features yourself.

- Reduce the lines of code needed for a program and make it more concise and readable.

- Encapsulate patterns and repetitive code and replace it with a simple macro call.

Want to add a new feature to the language to help make your life easier? In many languages, you are unable to do this yourself. To get a new language feature added, you must request or submit the change. Then the change has to be evaluated. After the evaluation, it needs to be tested. Finally, it can be used with a new version release of the language. All this takes *time*. With macros, you can just do it yourself. No wait, no fuss.

In fact, if you look closely, many Clojure core expressions are actually macros. This is the case with when. The following shows the source code for the when expression, which uses the defmacro form for creation:

```
(defmacro when ❶
  "Evaluates test. If logical true, evaluates body in an implicit do."
  {:added "1.0"} ❷
  [test & body]    ❸
  (list 'if test (cons 'do body)))  ❹
```

❶ defmacro is used to create a macro called when.

❷ A map describing when it was added to the language.

❸ It takes as arguments a logical test and treats the other args as the body of the expression.

❹ A list of the code is returned. This list is actually code. It constructs an if statement with the test and wraps the body in a do (which evaluates the expression for side effects like printing).

The when macro is creating code *from code*. It is using the fact the *code is data* in Clojure. The macro takes the code in and transforms it to new code for the program to evaluate.

Another tool to help see what is going on here is the macroexpand function. It takes a macro form and allows us to see what the code will look like once the macro is done transforming it.

For example, this example code for when prints a string when evaluated:

```
(when (= 2 2) (println "It is four!"))

;; prints "It is four!" to the stdout
```

We can see *how* it will evaluate the code using macroexpand-1. When using macroexpand-1, we need to quote the code that we want to take a look at. This is so that the code will be treated as data rather than being run as a function. In this case, we are quoting the when form:

```
(macroexpand-1
  '(when (= 2 2) (println "It is four!")))
;; -> (if (= 2 2)
;;      (do (println "It is four!")))
```

Now that we have seen what a macro looks like, we can try creating one for ourselves. One good reason to use macros is to encapsulate patterns and repetitive code, replacing it with a more concise macro call. Let's look at a case where this would be useful. We are going to be refactoring some already existing code to be better.

Creating Our Own Macros

We have some already written code about the characters from *Alice in Wonderland*. What this code does is introduce the characters to the Queen of Hearts. They always do so politely because she is constantly looking for excuses to cut people's heads off:

```
(defn hi-queen [phrase] ❶
  (str phrase ", so please your Majesty."))

(defn alice-hi-queen [] ❷
  (hi-queen "My name is Alice"))

(alice-hi-queen) ❸
;; -> "My name is Alice, so please your Majesty."

(defn march-hare-hi-queen [] ❹
  (hi-queen "I'm the March Hare"))

(march-hare-hi-queen) ❺
;; -> "I'm the March Hare, so please your Majesty."

(defn white-rabbit-hi-queen [] ❻
  (hi-queen "I'm the White Rabbit"))

(white-rabbit-hi-queen) ❼
;; -> "I'm the White Rabbit, so please your Majesty."

(defn mad-hatter-hi-queen [] ❽
  (hi-queen "I'm the Mad Hatter"))

(mad-hatter-hi-queen) ❾
;; -> "I'm the Mad Hatter, so please your Majesty."
```

❶ We are defining a hi-queen function that will take in a phrase and return a polite response.

❷ The alice-hi-queen function uses the hi-queen function but adds "My name is Alice" as the input.

❸ When evaluated, the `alice-hi-queen` function gives the polite introduction.

❹ The `march-hare-hi-queen` function uses the phrase "I'm the March Hare" as the input.

❺ When evaluated, the `march-hare-hi-queen` function gives the polite introduction.

❻ The `white-rabbit-hi-queen` function uses the phrase "I'm the White Rabbit" as the input.

❼ When evaluated, the `white-rabbit-hi-queen` function gives the polite introduction.

❽ The `mad-hatter-hi-queen` function uses the phrase "I'm the Mad Hatter" as the input.

❾ When evaluated, the `mad-hatter-hi-queen` function gives the polite introduction.

Among all this repetition in the functions, we can see a pattern start to emerge:

- The function name is the character name with a hyphen and then "-hi-queen."
- The string of the character's introduction is returned with the polite "so please your Majesty."

If we have two pieces of data, the name of the symbol and the introduction, we could generate the function with a macro.

 Remember, Clojure symbols refer to values. When a symbol is evaluated, it returns the thing it refers to.

The best place to start when creating your own macro is the end. We need to visualize how we want to call our macro and what the code will look like once it is called. Once we know what we want the end result to look like, we can then concentrate on creating the transformation that we want the macro to do.

So before we write any code, we will first take an example and imagine what the end result will look like.

We want to be able to call our macro with the two pieces of information it needs—the symbol of the function and the introduction. Because the macro will be generating these functions, we will call it def-hi-queen. This is how we will want to call it:

```
(def-hi-queen alice-hi-queen "My name is Alice")
```

Imagine the end result. Once our imagined macro is evaluated, we want it to create the original alice-phrase function for us:

```
(defn alice-hi-queen []
  (hi-queen "My name is Alice"))
```

Knowing our end result, we can actually go about creating our macro with defmacro. We are going to create it with the knowledge that code is data and we can create a list with code that we want as an end result:

```
(defmacro def-hi-queen [name phrase] ❶
  (list 'defn ❷
        (symbol name) ❸
        [] ❹
        (list 'hi-queen phrase))) ❺
```

❶ We create the macro with the name def-hi-queen that takes two args: the function symbol name and the introduction.

❷ A list of code is the data that we return because *code is data*. The first element in the code list is the symbol for defn. We put a quote around it because we don't want to evaluate it in the macro, we want to return the symbol.

❸ Here we create a symbol from the name argument.

❹ This is a vector for the args that defn expects.

❺ We return a list with the quoted function hi-queen and the phrase introduction. It is quoted because we don't want to evaluate it during the time of the macro, but we want it to be part of the code that we return.

Having constructed our def-hi-queen macro, we can see what it will look like when we call it with an example in macro-expand-1:

```
(macroexpand-1 '(def-hi-queen alice-hi-queen "My name is Alice"))
;; -> (defn alice-hi-queen []
;;       (hi-queen "My name is Alice"))
```

That looks exactly like what we need. We can actually evaluate this macro and it will create the alice-hi-queen function for us:

```
(def-hi-queen alice-hi-queen "My name is Alice")
;; -> #'user/alice-hi-queen
```

And we can now call the `alice-hi-queen` function ourselves:

```
(alice-hi-queen)
;; -> "My name is Alice, so please your Majesty."
```

We can now refactor the orginal code and get rid of the repetitive code and replace it with our macro:

```
(defmacro def-hi-queen [name phrase]
  (list 'defn
        (symbol name)
        []
        (list 'hi-queen phrase)))
;; -> #'user/def-hi-queen

(def-hi-queen alice-hi-queen "My name is Alice")
;; -> #'user/alice-hi-queen
(def-hi-queen march-hare-hi-queen "I'm the March Hare")
;; -> #'user/march-hare-hi-queen
(def-hi-queen white-rabbit-hi-queen "I'm the White Rabbit")
;; -> #'user/white-rabbit-hi-queen
(def-hi-queen mad-hatter-hi-queen "I'm the Mad Hatter")
;; -> #'user/mad-hatter-hi-queen
```

All the functions were created for us by the macro, so we can use them:

```
(alice-hi-queen)
;; -> "My name is Alice, so please your Majesty."

(march-hare-hi-queen)
;; -> "I'm the March Hare, so please your Majesty."

(white-rabbit-hi-queen)
;; -> "I'm the White Rabbit, so please your Majesty."

(mad-hatter-hi-queen)
;; -> "I'm the Mad Hatter, so please your Majesty."
```

There is another way we could have created this macro to make it even more concise: using a technique called *templating*.

Using Templating to Create Macros

Templating in Clojure uses something called the *Syntax-quote*. You can recognize it by the ` (or *backtick*) before the code. It works very similar to the regular quote, in that it returns the code as data in a list form.

Here is a list of code with the regular quote:

```
'(first [1 2 3])
;; -> (first [1 2 3])
```

Here is a list of code using the Syntax-quote:

```
`(first [1 2 3])
;; -> (clojure.core/first [1 2 3])
```

One difference to notice is that the symbol for the `first` function is fully qualified. The other difference is that we can use the Syntax-quote in combination with another templating helper called the *Unquote*, which is represented by the tilde (~). Using them together, we can insert values into the syntax quote. This gives us finer control over what the resulting code will look like.

With just a plain Syntax-quote, we can't get the value of x in the following code into the resulting list. This is because the Syntax-quote prevents evaluation like the regular quote:

```
(let [x 5]
  `(first [x 2 3]))
;; -> (clojure.core/first [user/x 2 3])
```

The code returned has the symbol for x, but we really want the value 5 in there instead. This is where we can use the Unquote to tell that for the symbol of x, we actually want to use the value of it:

```
(let [x 5]
  `(first [~x 2 3]))
;; -> (clojure.core/first [5 2 3])
```

With the templating tools of the Syntax-quote and Unquote, we can rewrite our `def-hi-queen` macro into a more concise and readable form, without having to be contained in a list:

```
(defmacro def-hi-queen [name phrase]
  `(defn ~(symbol name) []  ❶
     (hi-queen ~phrase)))
```

❶ We use the ` (Syntax-quote) to quote the `defn` form. To get the name of the function, we use the ~ (Unquote) to evaluate the symbol of the name parameter.

Checking this with our `macroexpand-1`, we can see that it is doing the right thing:

```
(macroexpand-1 '(def-hi-queen alice-hi-queen "My name is Alice"))
;; -> (clojure.core/defn alice-hi-queen []
;;      (user/hi-queen "My name is Alice"))
```

We can then use it as our `def-hi-queen` macro:

```
(def-hi-queen dormouse-hi-queen "I am the Dormouse")
;; -> #'user/dormouse-hi-queen

(dormouse-hi-queen)
;; -> "I am the Dormouse, so please your Majesty."
```

You now know the basics of Clojure macros.

Macros are powerful, but they come with a cost. Because they use meta-programming, they are not as easy to understand as a regular function. They are also harder to compose. For instance, you can't use them directly with a higher-order function like `map` or `filter`. It is a good rule to never write a macro if you can use a regular function instead.

 Don't use a macro unless you have to.

So when exactly do you need to use them? You need macros to overcome the limitation of functions *when* code is evaluated. With functions, the parameters are always eagerly evaluated. This is the case in the `when` macro. It has a parameters that are used in a control structure that we do not want to eagerly evaluate. Another reason to use a macro is if you have some code that you want to be evaluated when the macro is evaluated, at *compile time*, rather than *runtime* when functions are evaluated. Finally, another good reason to use a macro is if you want a custom syntax that cannot be evaluated with the normal function's syntax. In this case, you need to transform the functions, syntax before you can call them.

It is a good time to step back and review what you have learned about macros so far:

- Macros are a way of meta-programming in Clojure
- The benefits of using macros for concise code, pattern encapsulation, and language features
- How to create a macro using `defmacro` and plain lists
- How to create a macro using `defmacro` and templating
- The great power you wield with macros, and how to use it sparingly

With macros under your belt, you have completed our guided tour of Clojure. You have also finished the first part of the book. You now have all the skills you need to start Part II, where the *Living Clojure* Training Program starts. This is where your new skills will get a pratice plan, your brain will get used to a new way of thinking, and you will start *living Clojure*.

> *Oh, I've had such a curious dream!*
>
> —Alice in Wonderland

Living Clojure Training Program

Welcome to the second part of the book. While Part I of the book was dedicated to getting you up and running with a guided tour of Clojure, this is where you make it your own. We will be focused on a structured training program that is designed to give your brain practice and time to grow and think in this new way.

Learning a new language is not unlike learning how to run. You are getting your brain used to thinking in a new way. Beginning runners often encounter problems because they trying to do *too much too fast*. While my previous attempts at running failed, I finally had luck with Couch to 5K, an app that provides a gradual training program over a period of weeks. It helped me conquer the problem of trying to take on too much and getting overwhelmed. People try to do *too much too fast* when learning a new language, too. This *Living Clojure* Training Program uses the technique of a gradual training plan structured over the course of seven weeks. By the end, you will be comfortable and confident thinking Clojure. Even more important, you will have the tools and resources that will plug you into the community, so that you can grow and *live* Clojure.

CHAPTER 9

Joining the Clojure Community

Before starting the training program, you will need some resources to help you on your way. These resources will not only help you with the training program, but they will help you continue to live and grow with Clojure. They will get you hooked into the Clojure Community.

One of the first questions you might have is where to find online documentation about the Clojure language.

Clojure Documentation

There are some really good online sources of documentation and language reference. Let's take a quick tour of them.

The first site is *http://clojuredocs.org/*, the home of Clojure Documentation. It is community driven and incredibly useful to beginners.

ClojureDocs

ClojureDocs allows you to look up a Clojure function or macro by name. For example, if you couldn't remember exactly how to use the comp function, you could type it into the search area in ClojureDocs, as shown in Figure 9-1.

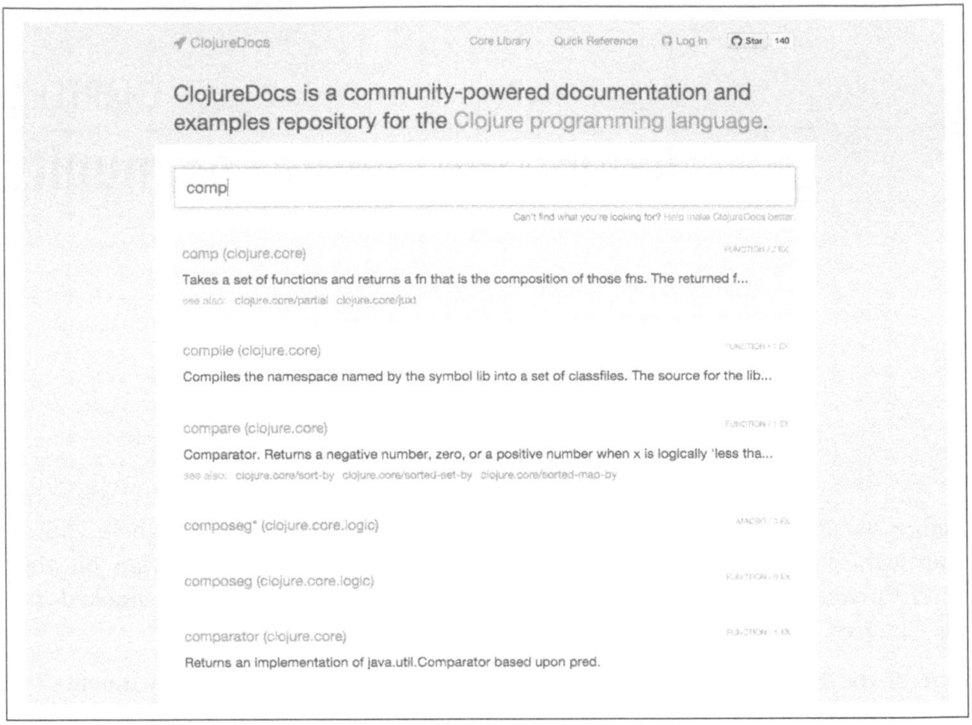

Figure 9-1. ClojureDocs search

You can then go to the reference docs for that function. It will give you a description of the function along with the arguments that it takes. There is also a link to the source code. Best of all, there are example usages.

The *see also* section is also really useful, especially when you are just getting started. It allows you to discover new functions when you want to do something similar to a function you already know. It is also a good tool to find a function when you forget its name. For example, you can find `doall` or `dorun` from the *see also* section of *doseq*.

Another great feature is the Quick Reference (*http://clojuredocs.org/quickref*). It is basically a nice overview/cheat sheet for the language. This is very handy if you are browsing for a particular feature in the language but you don't know the name. For example, you can see what content tests there are for collections. You could go to the QuickReference docs and look at the Simple Values section, as shown in Figure 9-2.

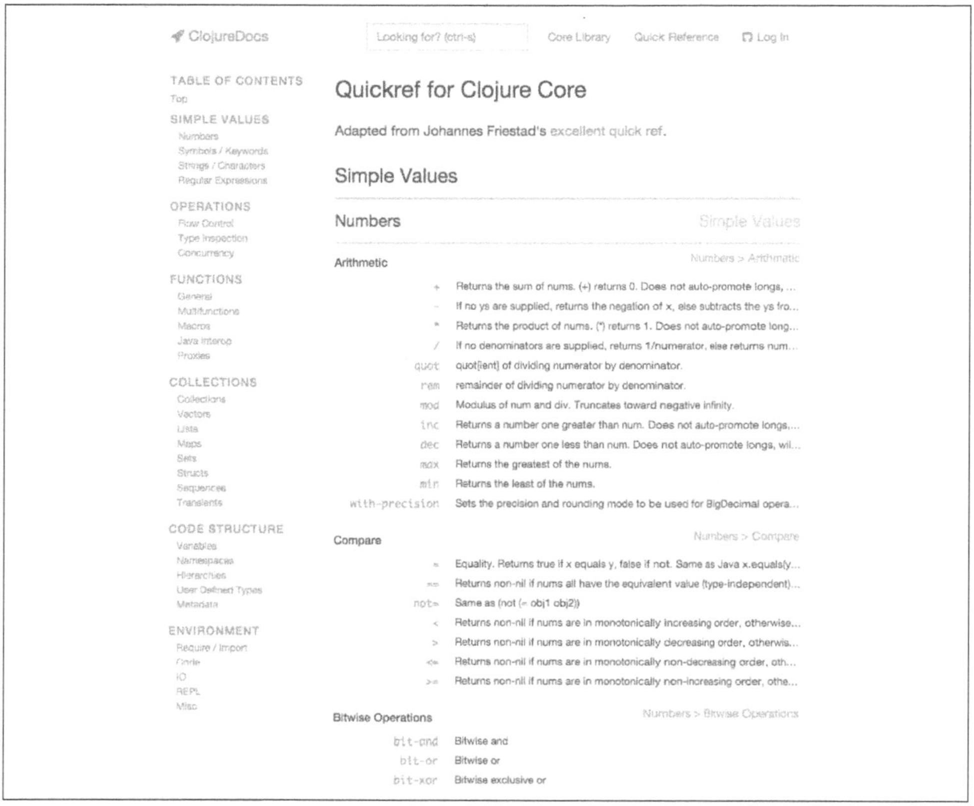

Figure 9-2. ClojureDocs Quick Ref

You can also browse ClojureDocs by namespace. You might want to do this when you are looking for functions in a certain area. For example, if you want to see what functions are available in the `clojure.set` namespace, you can click the Core Library (*http://clojuredocs.org/core-library*) link on the top and then choose the namespace you are interested in on the side of the page. You will see the functions in `clojure.set`, as shown in Figure 9-3.

Figure 9-3. ClojureDocs namespace browse

Being community driven, it is *living documentation*. It is continually updated and it grows as the language grows. You can also make it better. If you see any areas that need more examples, feel free to contribute and make it better for everyone.

Another good site for Clojure documentation is called Grimoire (*http://conj.io*).

Grimoire

Grimoire enables you to search for functions and see code examples. The nice thing about Grimoire is that a one-page cheatsheet/overview of the language is on the main page. The streamlined simplicity of the site, as you can see in Figure 9-4, makes it very easy to find the answers you want.

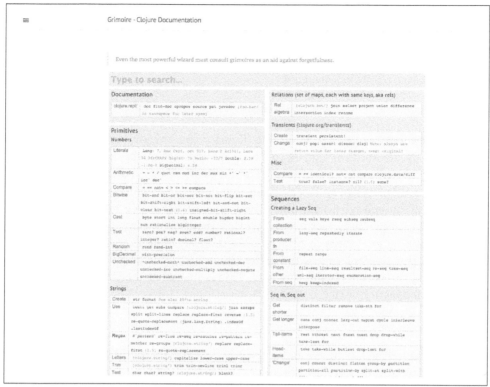

Figure 9-4. Grimoire website

Going to the source is the ultimate way to figure out how a function or macro works.

Going to the Source

There are a few ways to look at the source code for Clojure. As we mentioned earlier, documentation sites like ClojureDocs link to the source code in the documentation. You could also go straight to Clojure's GitHub (*https://github.com/clojure/clojure*) and browse all the source code yourself at any time. Even better, some editors, like Emacs, have command keys that let you jump directly to the source code. This a very convenient way to get documentation without ever having to leave the comfort of your editor. It is worth taking a couple minutes to check how to do this in your chosen editor.

We have talked about where to look for documentation on the Clojure language itself, but what about Clojure libraries? What if you are looking for a Clojure SQL or Redis library? Where can you go to find out what libraries are out there?

Which Libraries to Use

There are some good online resources that will help you discover Clojure libraries and decide which ones are best to use. We have already talked about the Clojars (*https://clojars.org/*) site in Chapter 4.

Clojars

Clojars is a good way to look at specific libraries you already know about. You can also search by keyword on Clojars to find a library that might match what you are looking for. For example, if you need to find a Redis client, you could search by the `redis` keyword and discover libraries with that name. Then you could look at each of them on GitHub and see which one is best for you. Searching by name on Clojars might work in some cases, but it won't work if the library name doesn't match what you are searching for. In this case, there is another way to look at which Clojure libraries to use. You can look across the *entire* Clojure ecosystem and see which are the most used libraries across other projects. This is just what the site CrossClj (*http://crossclj.info/*) does.

CrossClj

The CrossClj website (as shown in Figure 9-5), lets you see all the libraries in Clojars color coded by how they are used in other projects.

The darker the color of the library, the more it is used by others. This will give you a good feeling for how mature a library is before you decide to use it in your project. You can also search by project, namespace, or function name. A really cool feature is the ability to search for a function name across all the libraries. For example, you could see how many people are using the `reduce` function. You can also do a full-text search in the complete documentation of all projects (*http://crossclj.info/docs.html*). An example of this would be if you need a library to work with *redis*. You can search on the term and find all the places in the libraries and functions where the word is mentioned.

Figure 9-5. CrossClj website

Two other resources to use when looking for good libraries are ClojureWerkz (*http://clojurewerkz.org/*) and the Clojure Toolbox (*http://www.clojure-toolbox.com/*).

ClojureWerkz and the Clojure Toolbox

The ClojureWerkz site hosts a collection of high-quality open source libraries that were designed to make life easier using Clojure for practical purposes. The site was created by and is maintained by the authors of all these libraries, so it's a great place to check out, as you can see in Figure 9-6.

Figure 9-6. ClojureWerkz website

The Clojure Toolbox (*http://www.clojure-toolbox.com/*) is also a great site that has a directory listing of popular Clojure libraries, as shown in Figure 9-7.

It doesn't stop there—many great Clojure libraries are available. The Clojure community is very active and there are new exciting libraries being created all the time. Where do you go for news?

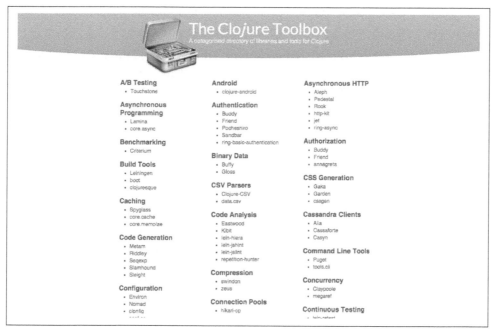

The Clojure Toolbox
A categorised directory of libraries and tools for Clojure

A/B Testing
- Touchstone

Asynchronous Programming
- Lamina
- core.async

Benchmarking
- Criterium

Build Tools
- Leiningen
- boot
- clojuresque

Caching
- Spyglass
- core.cache
- core.memoize

Code Generation
- Metam
- Riddley
- Seqexp
- Slamhound
- Sleight

Configuration
- Environ
- Nomad
- clonfig

Android
- clojure-android

Authentication
- Buddy
- Friend
- Pocheshiro
- Sandbar
- ring-basic-authentication

Binary Data
- Buffy
- Gloss

CSV Parsers
- Clojure-CSV
- data.csv

Code Analysis
- Eastwood
- Kibit
- lein-hiera
- lein-jshint
- lein-jslint
- repetition-hunter

Compression
- swindon
- zeus

Connection Pools
- hikari-cp

Asynchronous HTTP
- Aleph
- Pedestal
- Rook
- http-kit
- jet
- ring-async

Authorization
- Buddy
- Friend
- annagreta

CSS Generation
- Gaka
- Garden
- cssgen

Cassandra Clients
- Alia
- Cassaforte
- Casyn

Command Line Tools
- Puget
- tools.cli

Concurrency
- Claypoole
- megaref

Continuous Testing
- lein-retest

Figure 9-7. Clojure Toolbox website

Clojure News

New and exciting things in Clojure are happening so fast, you might wonder how to keep up. With the pace of change, you need to know where to look to find out about brand-new libraries and upcoming changes to existing ones. In general, where do you go to find out what is happening in the Clojure ecosystem? There are a number of good places to stay up with the latest news in the Clojure world. The first place to mention is the Clojure mailing list (*https://groups.google.com/forum/#!forum/clojure*). It is hosted on Google Groups and is very active. You will find announcements about Clojure libraries here, as well as news on the Clojure language. Joining is a great way to get plugged in to what is going on in the Clojure world.

While the Clojure mailing list is great, it doesn't include everthing that is going on. People are exploring ideas in blog posts and videos every day.

You can find blog news on the Clojure blog aggregator Planet Clojure (*http://planet.clojure.in/*).

If you want to keep up on a daily basis via the firehose, you can check out the Clojure sub on Reddit (*http://www.reddit.com/r/Clojure/*). Users post tons of interesting things that are going on in and around the Clojure community.

The Clojure community is also active on Twitter. To find Clojure news, you simply need to search for the #clojure hashtag (*http://bit.ly/clojure_tag*).

If you want to integrate your Clojure news with other news and interests, I would recommend Prismatic (*http://getprismatic.com/*). It is a news service that has machine learning smarts and is plugged into Clojure news as well other news interests.

 Prismatic is also programmed in Clojure!

There is a weekly newsletter that will keep you informed of the highlights called The Clojure Gazette (*http://www.clojuregazette.com/*). Curated by Eric Normad, it helps to collect the highlights from diverse sources. It is a wonderful way to keep up with the high-signal Clojure items, without needing to follow the daily details. Other Clojure newsletters you might want to check out are (def newsletter) (*http://defnewsletter.com/*) and Clojure Weekly (*http://reborg.tumblr.com/*). Keeping up with news is important, but so is actually *connecting* with other Clojurists and sharing ideas. We want your ideas in the community, so let's talk about where to get connected with other people who are enthusiastic about Clojure.

Finding Other Clojurists

The Clojure mailing list and Twitter are great places to connect with other Clojurists and exchange ideas. Another good place is using the IRC #clojure chat channel on freenode.

Chat

If you haven't used IRC before, you might be wondering what it is. IRC is a network of chatrooms. A particular chatroom that you are interested in, like Clojure, is called a *channel*. These channels are hosted on servers. To join a channel, you will need to get an *IRC client*. There are many IRC clients, so feel free to look at which one you like the best. For starters, you can try LimeChat (*http://limechat.net/mac/*) for Mac, Konversation (*https://konversation.kde.org/*) for Linux, and mIRC (*http://www.mirc.com/*) for Windows. There is also a good tutorial on wikiHow (*http://bit.ly/getstarted_irc*). Some editors, like Emacs, even support IRC. Once you get the client, you will connect to the freenode server and join the #clojure channel. You can select your username and join in the conversation!

You can meet Clojurists from all around the world at Clojure conferences. They are wonderful places to connect with people in person and get inspired by great talks.

There are more conferences all the time with the increasing popularity of Clojure, but I will list a few of the bigger ones.

Conferences

- Clojure Conj (*http://clojure-conj.org/*) is the original Clojure Conference and still one of the best.
- Clojure/West (*http://www.clojurewest.org/*) is run by the same folks as Clojure Conj but on the West Coast.
- Euro Clojure (*http://euroclojure.org/*) is the biggest conf in Europe.
- Clojure eXchange (*https://skillsmatter.com/conferences*) has many quality talks in London.
- Strange Loop (*https://thestrangeloop.com/*) is a fantastic conference covering many languages, including Clojure. It's led by Alex Miller.
- Lambda Jam (*http://www.lambdajam.com/*) covers functional languages and has hands-on *jam* sessions built in.

If you get a chance, I highly recommend you going to one or more. It is a wonderful experience and will help get you plugged into the community.

Another advantage of getting involved in the Clojure community is having people to help you when you have questions or problems.

Getting Help with Problems and Questions

Sometimes you need a little help. Getting stuck on a problem is no fun, but luckily there are friendly Clojurists that you can turn to. The best place to find help depends on what your problem is, but here is a list of places to look:

IRC
> If you want to chat with someone and get an immediate answer, this is a great place to go. Many libraries also have their own channels for specific questions. You can check the GitHub project to see if one is listed.

Mailing List
> You can ask questions on the mailing list. The answers might not be as quick, but it might reach more people than the IRC channel. Many libraries also have their own mailing lists.

Twitter
> If your question can fit in a tweet, this is also a good option for a quick response.

StackOverflow
> Always a great resource and has a depth of Clojure answers.

GitHub Issues
> If you are having a problem with the library and it looks like it might be a bug, you can open an issue—or even better, if you find the answer, submit some code to fix it.

Being part of community not only gives you a way to get a helping hand, it also enables you to *create* and *build* things with others.

Building Things with Other Clojure Enthusiasts

This is one of my personal favorite ways to get involved in the community. You can learn Clojure and help build things with others at the same time. How do you get involved?

The first way is one we just mentioned. When you find a problem in a library, you can fix it and share it back. Using GitHub, you can do this by submitting a pull-request (*https://help.github.com/articles/using-pull-requests/*), which is a way to submit a code patch. You can also take this one step further, by proactively looking at active issues with a library and fixing problems that others have reported. You might also think of new ways that library could be improved and submit a pull request for a new feature.

 With new features, it is always good to talk your idea through with the project owner first. This makes sure that it meshes with the owner's ideas for the project and also gives you a chance to get valuable input *before* starting to code.

You can also get involved in helping out the Clojure language itself. You can find out more information about the contributing process on the Clojure contributing page (*http://clojure.org/contributing*). Basically, you just need to submit a *Contributor Agreement* (CA). You can then join the Clojure-Dev mailing list (*http://bit.ly/clojure-dev_group*) for discussing changes to the Clojure language.

Finally, you can start your own open source project. Let your creativity flow and make your Clojure application or library. Don't forget to announce it to the community on the mailing list, blog, or chat. Also, remember to clearly document not only what your project does, but also how people can build, test, and find the best ways to get involved with it.

Summary

One of the best things about Clojure is the community. Clojure is not only a language—it is an ecosystem made up of people, libraries, tools, and shared philosophy. Get plugged into the community and you will find an abundance of resources that will not only help your project, but yourself as a developer. It will help you *live* Clojure.

Now that you know how to join the community and find online resources, you are ready to move on to the final chapters of the book. This is where you will practice all of what you have learned in the *Living Clojure* Training Program.

CHAPTER 10

Weekly Living Clojure Training Plan

You have all the skills and tools you need to embark on the *Living Clojure* Training Program. This chapter provides a seven-week plan designed not only to get you more and more comfortable in the language, but also to get you involved with the great feedback and resources that the community has to offer.

How Do I Use This Training Plan?

The structured training plan spans seven weeks. Each week has five days of exercises to complete, which are designed to fit into your schedule. They should only take you about a half an hour to an hour a day. The important part is to practice your Clojure skills regularly over a period of time. This is what is going to get your brain comfortable thinking in a new way. The first three weeks will be focused on solving problems with the 4Clojure website. The next three weeks will then go on to solve project-based programming exercises inspired by Lewis Carroll and *Alice in Wonderland*. The last week is devoted to creating your own Clojure web app and hosting it on Heroku. For each week, there will be step-by-step instructions to get you started.

I know it is tempting to skip ahead and plow right through everything as fast as you can. You can certainly do it. But I suggest that you try sticking to the plan and don't do too much at once.

What If I Miss a Day or Two?

Don't worry about it too much. This is not a race. If you miss a day or two, just pick up where you left off and continue from there.

What If I Don't Understand the Exercise?

Don't worry. You will be fine. This book has you well prepared with the basics of Clojure. Not only that, you know where to look for documentation online and where to get help with problems and questions, as outlined in Chapter 9.

Also, at the beginning of each new training section, we will be doing a problem or two together to make sure you are comfortable, before doing the rest on your own.

What are we waiting for? Let's get started.

Week 1

We are going to be practicing Clojure with the help of a fantastic website called 4Clojure (*http://www.4clojure.com/*), shown in Figure 10-1.

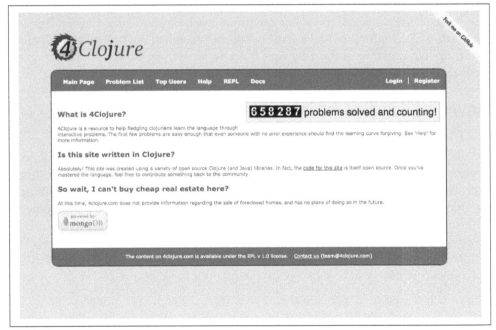

Figure 10-1. 4Clojure website

This site (which is built in Clojure) hosts code exercises in a *koan-style*, which broadly means *fill in the blanks*. Each exercise has one to many statements with blanks in them. Your goal is to fill in the blanks with the correct code that will make the statements true.

We will go through a couple problems together to get comfortable.

Go to the 4Clojure website and click the Problem List page. Select the first problem Nothing but the Truth (*https://www.4clojure.com/problem/1*). You will see the following:

This is a clojure form. Enter a value which will make the form evaluate to true. Don't over think it! If you are confused, see the getting started page. Hint: true is equal to true.

```
(= __ true)
```

We want to replace the blanks with something that makes the expression evaluate to true. In fact, *true* is the answer.

For this problem, *true* is already filled in for you in the code window on the bottom half of the web page, as shown in Figure 10-2.

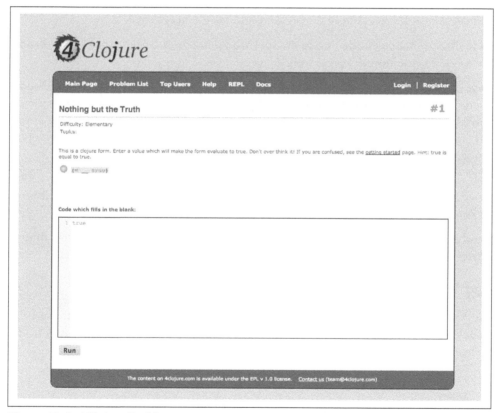

Figure 10-2. 4Clojure Problem 1

Click the green Run button to submit your answer. The website will run the tests against your solution and tell you that you have solved the problem. You can track your progress with a login. It is a good time to take a minute and register yourself now.

We will do another one together. This time choose Simple Math (*https://www.4clo jure.com/problem/2#prob-title*).

We need to solve the problem in the expression so that it will evaluate to true. The first thing we need to do is to see what the blank should be equal to.

```
(= (- 10 (* 2 3)) __)
```

Doing the math here.

- *(* 2 3) evaluates to 6*
- *Then (- 10 6) is 4*
- *We are looking for number to fill in the blank for (= 4)__*

The answer is 4. Click Run in the browser and see if you are right.

Actually, any statement that evaluates to 4 would also be a correct answer. For example (+ 2 2) would work just as well.

One of the nice things about the site is that once you are logged in you can follow users. This means that you can see other people's solutions to the problem once you solve it. It is a great way to learn by seeing how others approached the problem. If you get stuck and need some extra help solving a problem, you can also visit the 4Clojure Google Group (*http://bit.ly/4clojure_group*).

You can choose to do these problems directly on the website, work in your REPL, or even create your own Leiningen project to keep your solutions organized. It is up to you.

Ready? Let's start. Remember, the goal is to fill in the blanks (denoted by two underscores) with the code to make the statement true.

Day 1

We are starting off with some easy ones to get you warmed up. The exercise titles match up to the titles on the 4Clojure problems page; follow the URLs to go to the website and complete each exercise.

Useful areas for review:

- "Put Your Clojure Data in Collections" on page 6
- "Using Sets for Unique Collections of Data" on page 13
- "Handling Interop with Java" on page 69

Intro to Strings

Lesson URL: *https://www.4clojure.com/problem/3*

Clojure strings are Java strings. This means that you can use any of the Java string methods on Clojure strings.

```
(= __ (.toUpperCase "hello world"))
```

Intro to Lists

Lesson URL: *https://www.4clojure.com/problem/4*

Lists can be constructed with either a function or a quoted form.

```
(= (list __) '(:a :b :c))
```

Lists: conj

Lesson URL: *https://www.4clojure.com/problem/5*

When operating on a list, the conj function will return a new list with one or more items "added" to the front.

```
(= __ (conj '(2 3 4) 1))
```

```
(= __ (conj '(3 4) 2 1))
```

Intro to Vectors

Lesson URL: *https://www.4clojure.com/problem/6*

Vectors can be constructed several ways. You can compare them with lists.

```
(= [__]
   (list :a :b :c)
   (vec '(:a :b :c))
   (vector :a :b :c))
```

Vectors: conj

Lesson URL: *https://www.4clojure.com/problem/7*

When operating on a Vector, the conj function will return a new vector with one or more items "added" to the end.

```
(= __ (conj [1 2 3] 4))
```

```
(= __ (conj [1 2] 3 4))
```

Intro to Sets

Lesson URL: *https://www.4clojure.com/problem/8*

Sets are collections of unique values.

```
(= __ (set '(:a :a :b :c :c :c :c :d :d)))
```

```
(= __ (clojure.set/union #{:a :b :c} #{:b :c :d}))
```

Sets: conj

Lesson URL: *https://www.4clojure.com/problem/9*

When operating on a set, the conj function returns a new set with one or more keys "added".

```
(= #{1 2 3 4} (conj #{1 4 3} __))
```

Intro to Maps

Lesson URL: *https://www.4clojure.com/problem/10*

Maps store key-value pairs. Both maps and keywords can be used as lookup functions. Commas can be used to make maps more readable, but they are not required.

```
(= __ ((hash-map :a 10, :b 20, :c 30) :b))
```

```
(= __ (:b {:a 10, :b 20, :c 30}))
```

Maps: conj

Lesson URL: *https://www.4clojure.com/problem/11*

When operating on a map, the conj function returns a new map with one or more key-value pairs "added".

```
(= {:a 1, :b 2, :c 3} (conj {:a 1} __ [:c 3]))
```

Intro to Sequences

Lesson URL: *https://www.4clojure.com/problem/12*

All Clojure collections support sequencing. You can operate on sequences with functions like first, second, and last.

```
(= __ (first '(3 2 1)))
```

```
(= __ (second [2 3 4]))
```

```
(= __ (last (list 1 2 3)))
```

Day 2

Useful areas for review:

- "Creating Our Own Functions" on page 19
- "Symbols and the Art of Binding" on page 17
- "The Functional Shape of Data Transformations" on page 46

Sequences: rest

Lesson URL: *https://www.4clojure.com/problem/13*

The rest function will return all the items of a sequence except the first.

```
(= __ (rest [10 20 30 40]))
```

Intro to Functions

Lesson URL: *https://www.4clojure.com/problem/14*

Clojure has many different ways to create functions.

```
(= __ ((fn add-five [x] (+ x 5)) 3))

(= __ ((fn [x] (+ x 5)) 3))

(= __ (#(+ % 5) 3))

(= __ ((partial + 5) 3))
```

Double Down

Lesson URL: *https://www.4clojure.com/problem/15*

Write a function which doubles a number.

```
(= (__ 2) 4)

(= (__ 3) 6)

(= (__ 11) 22)

(= (__ 7) 14)
```

Hello World

Lesson URL: *https://www.4clojure.com/problem/16*

Write a function which returns a personalized greeting.

```
(= (__ "Dave") "Hello, Dave!")

(= (__ "Jenn") "Hello, Jenn!")

(= (__ "Rhea") "Hello, Rhea!")
```

Sequences: Maps

Lesson URL: *https://www.4clojure.com/problem/17*

The map function takes two arguments: a function (f) and a sequence (s). Map returns a new sequence consisting of the result of applying f to each item of s. Do not confuse the map function with the map data structure.

```
(= __ (map #(+ % 5) '(1 2 3)))
```

Sequences: filter

Lesson URL: *https://www.4clojure.com/problem/18*

The filter function takes two arguments: a predicate function (f) and a sequence (s). Filter returns a new sequence consisting of all the items of s for which (f item) returns true.

```
(= __ (filter #(> % 5) '(3 4 5 6 7)))
```

Local bindings

Lesson URL: *https://www.4clojure.com/problem/35*

Clojure lets you give local names to values using the special let-form.

```
(= __ (let [x 5] (+ 2 x)))

(= __ (let [x 3, y 10] (- y x)))

(= __ (let [x 21] (let [y 3] (/ x y))))
```

Let it Be

Lesson URL: *https://www.4clojure.com/problem/36*

Can you bind x, y, and z so that these are all true?

```
(= 10 (let __ (+ x y)))

(= 4 (let __ (+ y z)))

(= 1 (let __ z))
```

Day 3

Useful areas for review:

- "Recursion" on page 43
- "The Functional Shape of Data Transformations" on page 46

Regular Expressions

Lesson URL: *https://www.4clojure.com/problem/37*

Regular expressions in Clojure are prefixed by a "#". The `re-seq` function finds and returns a sequence of matches for a string. For example, if we want to find all the matches for "jam" in a string:

```
(re-seq #"jam" "I like jam in my jam ")
;; -> ("jam" "jam")
```

Regex patterns use *reader macro*, which is different from a regular macro. The reader maps certain special characters to special behavior. The "#" symbol followed by a double-quoted string tells the reader that it is a regex pattern.

We are also using the `apply` function here, which takes a function and applies it to an argument list:

```
(apply str [1 2 3])
;; -> "123"
```

Now, onto the problem.

Regex patterns are supported with a special reader macro.

```
(= __ (apply str (re-seq #"[A-Z]+" "bA1B3Ce ")))
```

Simple Recursion

Lesson URL: *https://www.4clojure.com/problem/57*

A recursive function is a function which calls itself. This is one of the fundamental techniques used in functional programming.

```
(= __ ((fn foo [x] (when (> x 0) (conj (foo (dec x)) x))) 5))
```

Recurring Theme

Lesson URL: *https://www.4clojure.com/problem/68*

Clojure only has one non-stack-consuming looping construct: recur. Either a function or a loop can be used as the recursion point. Either way, recur rebinds the bindings of the recursion point to the values it is passed. Recur must be called from the tail-position, and calling it elsewhere will result in an error.

 A *tail-position* is the place in an expression that would return a value. There are no more forms evaluated after the tail-position.

```
(= __
  (loop [x 5
         result []]
    (if (> x 0)
      (recur (dec x) (conj result (+ 2 x)))
      result)))
```

Rearranging Code: ->

https://www.4clojure.com/problem/71

This problem uses the `thread-first` macro, `->`. This makes code more readable by threading and expression through the forms. This really helps when you have deeply nested functions or transformations. For example, if you want to take the first element from a list, turn it into a string, and then turn that into uppercase, you could do this:

```
(.toUpperCase (str (first [:cat :dog :fish])))
;; -> ":CAT"
```

Using the `thread-first` macro, you can rewrite this as:

```
(-> [:cat :dog :fish] first str .toUpperCase)
;; -> ":CAT"
```

Use of this macro makes code more readable and concise.

The thread-first macro

> `->`

threads an expression x through a variable number of forms. First, x is inserted as the second item in the first form, making a list of it if it is not a list already. Then the first form is inserted as the second item in the second form, making a list of that form if necessary. This process continues for all the forms. Using thread-first can sometimes make your code more readable.

```
(= (__ (sort (rest (reverse [2 5 4 1 3 6])))))
    (-> [2 5 4 1 3 6] (reverse) (rest) (sort) (__))
    5)
```

Rearranging Code: ->>

Lesson URL: *https://www.4clojure.com/problem/72*

This problem uses the thread-last macro, ->>, which is much like the thread-first macro. ->> is much like the thread-first macro. The major difference is that it threads the expression as the last argument through the forms. This is especially useful if you want to use threading on collection functions like map, filter, and take where the collection is the last argument:

```
(->> [1 2 3 4 5 6 7 8] (filter even?) (take 3))
;; -> (2 4 6)
```

The thread-last macro threads an expression x through a variable number of forms. First, x is inserted as the last item in the first form, making a list of it if it is not a list already. Then the first form is inserted as the last item in the second form, making a list of that form if necessary. This process continues for all the forms. Using thread-last can sometimes make your code more readable.

```
(= (__ (map inc (take 3 (drop 2 [2 5 4 1 3 6])))))
   (->> [2 5 4 1 3 6] (drop 2) (take 3) (map inc) (__))
   11)
```

For the win

Lesson URL: *https://www.4clojure.com/problem/145*

Clojure's for macro is a tremendously versatile mechanism for producing a sequence based on some other sequence(s). It can take some time to understand how to use it properly, but that investment will be paid back with clear, concise sequence-wrangling later. With that in mind, read over these for expressions and try to see how each of them produces the same result.

```
(= __ (for [x (range 40)
            :when (= 1 (rem x 4))]
        x))

(= __ (for [x (iterate #(+ 4 %) 0)
            :let [z (inc x)]
            :while (< z 40)]
        z))

(= __ (for [[x y] (partition 2 (range 20))]
        (+ x y)))
```

Day 4

Useful areas for review:

- "Controlling the Flow with Logic" on page 26
- "The Functional Shape of Data Transformations" on page 46

Penultimate Element

Lesson URL: *https://www.4clojure.com/problem/20*

Write a function which returns the second to last element from a sequence.

```
(= (__ (list 1 2 3 4 5)) 4)

(= (__ ["a" "b" "c"]) "b")

(= (__ [[1 2] [3 4]]) [1 2])
```

Sum It All Up

Lesson URL: *https://www.4clojure.com/problem/24*

Write a function which returns the sum of a sequence of numbers.

```
(= (__ [1 2 3]) 6)

(= (__ (list 0 -2 5 5)) 8)

(= (__ #{4 2 1}) 7)

(= (__ '(0 0 -1)) -1)

(= (__ '(1 10 3)) 14)
```

Find the odd numbers

Lesson URL: *https://www.4clojure.com/problem/25*

Write a function which returns only the odd numbers from a sequence.

```
(= (__ #{1 2 3 4 5}) '(1 3 5))

(= (__ [4 2 1 6]) '(1))

(= (__ [2 2 4 6]) '())

(= (__ [1 1 1 3]) '(1 1 1 3))
```

Palindrome Detector

Lesson URL: *https://www.4clojure.com/problem/27*

Write a function which returns true if the given sequence is a palindrome. Hint: "race-car" does not equal '(\r \a \c \e \c \a \r)

```
(false? (__ '(1 2 3 4 5)))

(true? (__ "racecar"))

(true? (__ [:foo :bar :foo]))

(true? (__ '(1 1 3 3 1 1)))

(false? (__ '(:a :b :c)))
```

Duplicate a Sequence

Lesson URL: *https://www.4clojure.com/problem/32*

Write a function which duplicates each element of a sequence.

```
(= (__ [1 2 3]) '(1 1 2 2 3 3))

(= (__ [:a :a :b :b]) '(:a :a :a :a :b :b :b :b))

(= (__ [[1 2] [3 4]]) '([1 2] [1 2] [3 4] [3 4]))

(= (__ [[1 2] [3 4]]) '([1 2] [1 2] [3 4] [3 4]))
```

Day 5

Useful areas for review:

- "The Functional Shape of Data Transformations" on page 46

Compress a Sequence

Lesson URL: *https://www.4clojure.com/problem/30*

Write a function which removes consecutive duplicates from a sequence.

```
(= (apply str (__ "Leeeeeerrroyyy")) "Leroy")

(= (__ [1 1 2 3 3 2 2 3]) '(1 2 3 2 3))

(= (__ [[1 2] [1 2] [3 4] [1 2]]) '([1 2] [3 4] [1 2]))
```

Pack a Sequence

Lesson URL: *https://www.4clojure.com/problem/31*

Write a function which packs consecutive duplicates into sub-lists.

```
(= (__ [1 1 2 1 1 1 3 3]) '((1 1) (2) (1 1 1) (3 3)))

(= (__ [:a :a :b :b :c]) '((:a :a) (:b :b) (:c)))

(= (__ [[1 2] [1 2] [3 4]]) '(([1 2] [1 2]) ([3 4])))
```

Drop Every Nth Item

Lesson URL: *https://www.4clojure.com/problem/41*

Write a function which drops every Nth item from a sequence.

```
(= (__ [1 2 3 4 5 6 7 8] 3) [1 2 4 5 7 8])

(= (__ [:a :b :c :d :e :f] 2) [:a :c :e])

(= (__ [1 2 3 4 5 6] 4) [1 2 3 5 6])
```

Intro to Iterate

Lesson URL: *https://www.4clojure.com/problem/45*

The `iterate` function is one that makes an infinite lazy sequence. Remember to be careful with infinite sequences and use them with a `take`. The `iterate` function applies a function to an initial argument and then applies the same function to the result, and does it again, and again:

```
(take 5 (iterate inc 1))
;; -> (1 2 3 4 5)
```

The iterate function can be used to produce an infinite lazy sequence.

```
(= __ (take 5 (iterate #(+ 3 %) 1)))
```

Replicate a Sequence

Lesson URL: *https://www.4clojure.com/problem/33*

Write a function which replicates each element of a sequence a variable number of times.

```
(= (__ [1 2 3] 2) '(1 1 2 2 3 3))

(= (__ [:a :b] 4) '(:a :a :a :a :b :b :b :b))

(= (__ [4 5 6] 1) '(4 5 6))

(= (__ [[1 2] [3 4]] 2) '([1 2] [1 2] [3 4] [3 4]))
```

```
(= (__ [44 33] 2) [44 44 33 33])
```

Week 2

This week we are going to be continuing with more 4Clojure problems. They will be increasing in difficulty, giving you a good workout.

Day 1

 Useful areas for review:

- "Destructuring" on page 38
- "The Functional Shape of Data Transformations" on page 46

Fibonacci Sequence

Lesson URL: *https://www.4clojure.com/problem/26*

This problem has to do with *Fibonacci sequences*. It is a series of integers where the next number is found by adding up the two numbers before it:

```
0, 1, 1, 2, 3, 5, 8, 13, 21, 34, 55, 89, 144 ...
```

Write a function which returns the first X Fibonacci numbers.

```
(= (__ 3) '(1 1 2))
```

```
(= (__ 6) '(1 1 2 3 5 8))
```

```
(= (__ 8) '(1 1 2 3 5 8 13 21))
```

Get the Caps

Lesson URL: *https://www.4clojure.com/problem/29*

Write a function which takes a string and returns a new string containing only the capital letters.

```
(= (__ "HeLlO, WoRlD!") "HLOWRD")
```

```
(empty? (__ "nothing"))
```

```
(= (__ "$#A(*&987Zf") "AZ")
```

Intro to some

Lesson URL: *https://www.4clojure.com/problem/48*

The some function takes a predicate function and a collection. It returns the first logical true value of (predicate x) where x is an item in the collection.

```
(= __ (some #{2 7 6} [5 6 7 8]))
```

```
(= __ (some #(when (even? %) %) [5 6 7 8]))
```

Factorial Fun

Lesson URL: *https://www.4clojure.com/problem/42*

A factorial is a product of all positive integers less than or equal to *n*. An example is:

```
6! = 6 x 5 x 4 x 3 x 2 x 1 = 720
```

Write a function which calculates factorials.

```
(= (__ 1) 1)
```

```
(= (__ 3) 6)
```

```
(= (__ 5) 120)
```

```
(= (__ 8) 40320)
```

Intro to Destructuring

Lesson URL: *https://www.4clojure.com/problem/52*

Let bindings and function parameter lists support destructuring.

```
(= [2 4] (let [[a b c d e f g] (range)] __))
```

Day 2

Useful areas for review:

- "Controlling the Flow with Logic" on page 26
- "Destructuring" on page 38
- "The Functional Shape of Data Transformations" on page 46

Advanced Destructuring

Lesson URL: *https://www.4clojure.com/problem/51*

With destructuring, there are some advanced techniques. One is to use the ampersand to collect all the arguments after it into one binding. This example destructures a vector into bindings.

The first two bindings are the first two elements of the vector:

```
(let [[a b & c] ["cat" "dog" "bird" "fish"]]
  [a b])
;; -> ["cat" "dog"]
```

All the rest of the elements after the first two are bound to `c`:

```
(let [[a b & c] ["cat" "dog" "bird" "fish"]]
  c)
;; -> ("bird" "fish")
```

The other type of destructuring technique is to use the `:as` keyword. This takes the whole destructuring argument and binds it to a name:

```
(let [[a b :as x] ["cat" "dog" "bird" "fish"]]
  x)
;; -> ["cat" "dog" "bird" "fish"]
```

Now try this problem.

Here is an example of some more sophisticated destructuring.

```
(= [1 2 [3 4 5] [1 2 3 4 5]] (let [[a b & c :as d] __] [a b c d]))
```

A Half-Truth

Lesson URL: *https://www.4clojure.com/problem/83*

Write a function which takes a variable number of booleans. Your function should return true if some of the parameters are true, but not all of the parameters are true. Otherwise your function should return false.

```
(= false (__ false false))

(= true (__ true false))

(= false (__ true))

(= true (__ false true false))

(= false (__ true true true))

(= true (__ true true true false))
```

Greatest Common Divisor

Lesson URL: *https://www.4clojure.com/problem/66*

The greatest common divisor (gcd) is the largest positive integer that divides two numbers without a remainder.

Given two integers, write a function which returns the greatest common divisor.

```
(= (__ 2 4) 2)

(= (__ 10 5) 5)

(= (__ 5 7) 1)

(= (__ 1023 858) 33)
```

Day 3

Useful areas for review:

- "Using Sets for Unique Collections of Data" on page 13
- "Creating Our Own Functions" on page 19
- "The Functional Shape of Data Transformations" on page 46

Simple closures

Lesson URL: *https://www.4clojure.com/problem/107*

Lexical scope and first-class functions are two of the most basic building blocks of a functional language like Clojure. When you combine the two together, you get something very powerful called **lexical closures**. *With these, you can exercise a great deal of control over the lifetime of your local bindings, saving their values for use later, long after the code you're running now has finished.*

It can be hard to follow in the abstract, so let's build a simple closure. Given a positive integer n, return a function (f x) which computes x raised to the power n. Observe that the effect of this is to preserve the value of n for use outside the scope in which it is defined.

```
(= 256 ((__ 2) 16) ((__ 8) 2))

(= [1 8 27 64] (map (__ 3) [1 2 3 4]))

(= [1 2 4 8 16] (map #((__ %) 2) [0 1 2 3 4]))
```

Cartesian Product

Lesson URL: *https://www.4clojure.com/problem/90*

Write a function which calculates the Cartesian product (http://en.wikipedia.org/wiki/Cartesian_product) of two sets.

The online version has nice unicode hearts and symbols, which unfortunately don't show up in the printed code. The following code has the symbols substituted with text:

```
(= (__ #{"ace" "king" "queen"} #{"spade" "heart" "diamond" "club"})
  #{["ace"   "spade"] ["ace"   "heart"] ["ace"   "diamond"] ["ace"   "club"]
    ["king"  "spade"] ["king"  "heart"] ["king"  "diamond"] ["king"  "club"]
    ["queen" "spade"] ["queen" "heart"] ["queen" "diamond"] ["queen" "club"]})

(= (__ #{1 2 3} #{4 5})
  #{[1 4] [2 4] [3 4] [1 5] [2 5] [3 5]})

(= 300 (count (__ (into #{} (range 10))
                  (into #{} (range 30)))))
```

Day 4

Useful areas for review:

- "Using Sets for Unique Collections of Data" on page 13
- "Creating Our Own Functions" on page 19

Symmetric Difference

Lesson URL: *https://www.4clojure.com/problem/88*

Write a function which returns the symmetric difference of two sets. The symmetric difference is the set of items belonging to one but not both of the two sets.

```
(= (__ #{1 2 3 4 5 6} #{1 3 5 7}) #{2 4 6 7})

(= (__ #{:a :b :c} #{}) #{:a :b :c})

(= (__ #{} #{4 5 6}) #{4 5 6})

(= (__ #{[1 2] [2 3]} #{[2 3] [3 4]}) #{[1 2] [3 4]})
```

Least Common Multiple

Lesson URL: *https://www.4clojure.com/problem/100*

Write a function which calculates the least common multiple. (http://en.wikipedia.org/wiki/Least_common_multiple) Your function should accept a variable number of positive integers or ratios.

```
(== (__ 2 3) 6)

(== (__ 5 3 7) 105)

(== (__ 1/3 2/5) 2)

(== (__ 3/4 1/6) 3/2)

(== (__ 7 5/7 2 3/5) 210)
```

Day 5

Useful areas for review:

- "Recursion" on page 43
- "The Functional Shape of Data Transformations" on page 46

Pascal's Triangle

Lesson URL: *https://www.4clojure.com/problem/97*

Pascal's triangle (http://en.wikipedia.org/wiki/Pascal%27s_triangle) is a triangle of numbers computed using the following rules:

- *The first row is 1.*
- *Each successive row is computed by adding together adjacent numbers in the row above, and adding a 1 to the beginning and end of the row.*

Write a function which returns the nth row of Pascal's Triangle.

```
(= (__ 1) [1])

(= (map __ (range 1 6))
   [      [1]
         [1 1]
        [1 2 1]
       [1 3 3 1]
      [1 4 6 4 1]])
```

```
(= (__ 11)
   [1 10 45 120 210 252 210 120 45 10 1])
```

Week 3

This is our last week of doing 4Clojure problems. It's designed to give you a fun Clojure challenge each day.

Useful areas for review for all days:

- "Controlling the Flow with Logic" on page 26
- "Recursion" on page 43
- "The Functional Shape of Data Transformations" on page 46

If you need help solving a problem, visit the 4Clojure Google Group (*https://groups.google.com/forum/#!forum/4clojure*).

Day 1

To Tree, or not to Tree

Lesson URL: *https://www.4clojure.com/problem/95*

Write a predicate which checks whether or not a given sequence represents a binary tree (http://en.wikipedia.org/wiki/Binary_tree). Each node in the tree must have a value, a left child, and a right child.

```
(= (__ '(:a (:b nil nil) nil))
   true)

(= (__ '(:a (:b nil nil)))
   false)

(= (__ [1 nil [2 [3 nil nil] [4 nil nil]]])
   true)

(= (__ [1 [2 nil nil] [3 nil nil] [4 nil nil]])
   false)

(= (__ [1 [2 [3 [4 nil nil] nil] nil] nil])
   true)

(= (__ [1 [2 [3 [4 false nil] nil] nil] nil])
   false)

(= (__ '(:a nil ()))
   false)
```

Beauty is Symmetry

Lesson URL: *https://www.4clojure.com/problem/96*

Let us define a binary tree as "symmetric" if the left half of the tree is the mirror image of the right half of the tree. Write a predicate to determine whether or not a given binary tree is symmetric. (see To Tree, or not to Tree (https://www.4clojure.com/problem/95) for a reminder on the tree representation we're using).

```
(= (__ '(:a (:b nil nil) (:b nil nil))) true)

(= (__ '(:a (:b nil nil) nil)) false)

(= (__ '(:a (:b nil nil) (:c nil nil))) false)

(= (__ [1 [2 nil [3 [4 [5 nil nil] [6 nil nil]] nil]]
        [2 [3 nil [4 [6 nil nil] [5 nil nil]]] nil]])
   true)

(= (__ [1 [2 nil [3 [4 [5 nil nil] [6 nil nil]] nil]]
        [2 [3 nil [4 [5 nil nil] [6 nil nil]]] nil]])
   false)

(= (__ [1 [2 nil [3 [4 [5 nil nil] [6 nil nil]] nil]]
        [2 [3 nil [4 [6 nil nil] nil]] nil]])
   false)
```

Day 2

Flipping out

Lesson URL: *https://www.4clojure.com/problem/46*

Write a higher-order function which flips the order of the arguments of an input function.

```
(= 3 ((__ nth) 2 [1 2 3 4 5]))

(= true ((__ >) 7 8))

(= 4 ((__ quot) 2 8))

(= [1 2 3] ((__ take) [1 2 3 4 5] 3))
```

Rotate a sequence

Lesson URL: *https://www.4clojure.com/problem/44*

Write a function which can rotate a sequence in either direction.

```
(= (__ 2 [1 2 3 4 5]) '(3 4 5 1 2))

(= (__ -2 [1 2 3 4 5]) '(4 5 1 2 3))

(= (__ 6 [1 2 3 4 5]) '(2 3 4 5 1))

(= (__ 1 '(:a :b :c)) '(:b :c :a))

(= (__ -4 '(:a :b :c)) '(:c :a :b))
```

Day 3

The `interleave` function in Clojure is a lazy sequence of the first element of the first collection, the first element of the second collection, then the second of each, and on and on:

```
(interleave ["cat" "dog" "fish"] [1 2 3])
;; -> ("cat" 1 "dog" 2 "fish" 3)
```

This problem has to do with doing the *reverse* of `interleave`. That is, given a collection, break it up into subsequences that would have been used in an `interleave`.

Reverse Interleave

Lesson URL: *https://www.4clojure.com/problem/43*

Write a function which reverses the interleave process into x number of subsequences.

```
(= (__ [1 2 3 4 5 6] 2) '((1 3 5) (2 4 6)))

(= (__ (range 9) 3) '((0 3 6) (1 4 7) (2 5 8)))

(= (__ (range 10) 5) '((0 5) (1 6) (2 7) (3 8) (4 9)))
```

Split by Type

Lesson URL: *https://www.4clojure.com/problem/50*

Write a function which takes a sequence consisting of items with different types and splits them up into a set of homogeneous sub-sequences. The internal order of each sub-sequence should be maintained, but the sub-sequences themselves can be returned in any order (this is why set is used in the test cases).

```
(= (set (__ [1 :a 2 :b 3 :c])) #{[1 2 3] [:a :b :c]})

(= (set (__ [:a "foo" "bar" :b])) #{[:a :b] ["foo" "bar"]})

(= (set (__ [[1 2] :a [3 4] 5 6 :b])) #{[[1 2] [3 4]] [:a :b] [5 6]})
```

Day 4

Prime Numbers

Lesson URL: *https://www.4clojure.com/problem/67*

Write a function which returns the first x number of prime numbers.

```
(= (__ 2) [2 3])

(= (__ 5) [2 3 5 7 11])

(= (last (__ 100)) 541)
```

Day 5

Anagram Finder

Lesson URL: *https://www.4clojure.com/problem/77*

Write a function which finds all the anagrams in a vector of words. A word x is an anagram of word y if all the letters in x can be rearranged in a different order to form y. Your function should return a set of sets, where each sub-set is a group of words which are anagrams of each other. Each sub-set should have at least two words. Words without any anagrams should not be included in the result.

```
(= (__ ["meat" "mat" "team" "mate" "eat"])
   #{#{"meat" "team" "mate"}})

(= (__ ["veer" "lake" "item" "kale" "mite" "ever"])
   #{#{"veer" "ever"} #{"lake" "kale"} #{"mite" "item"}})
```

Week 4

This week, we are going to change gears a bit. We are going to continue our exercises doing programming *katas*. Programming katas are small, focused exercises that help build the skill of the developer. They differ from koans in that the scope is a bit larger. This time, you have an entire Leiningen project for each exercise. This means that you can start to explore and use other libraries to help you. Also, the tests are not static. Feel free to add tests and change them to fit your needs. You will run the tests to make them pass, so you will be able to practice your skills with Clojure testing.

The katas we are doing are called *Wonderland Clojure Katas* and can all be found at the GitHub repo *https://github.com/gigasquid/wonderland-clojure-katas*. They are a collection of katas inspired by Lewis Carroll and *Alice in Wonderland*.

To get started doing them on your own system, you will need to install Git, which is a version control system used by GitHub. You can find instructions on how to download it on your system at *https://help.github.com/articles/set-up-git/*.

Once you have Git installed on your system, you can go to a command line and type:

```
git clone https://github.com/gigasquid/wonderland-clojure-katas.git
```

This will copy the code repository with all the katas to a directory on your system called *wonderland-clojure-katas*. You can also just download the zipped version of repository if you prefer; it will work just fine.

Before we get started, just a reminder to do these at your own pace. They are *your katas* now. Generally, there are two days allocated for each kata. But if you need more time, take it. Likewise, if you finish up really quickly, maybe it is time to step back and think how you might refactor and improve it. The main point is to give your brain regular practice in the Clojure way of thinking.

If you need help or get stuck, there is a solutions section for each kata where people have shared their code. Try not to peek at them ahead of time. But if you need a pointer or hint, the code is there to help you.

Now, we can move on to our first kata of the week.

Day 1

We are going to start off with the *Alphabet Cipher* kata. Lewis Carroll published this cipher.

The *Alphabet Cipher* involves alphabet substitution using a keyword.

First, you must make a substitution chart like this, where each row of the alphabet is rotated by one as each letter goes down the chart:

```
  ABCDEFGHIJKLMNOPQRSTUVWXYZ
A abcdefghijklmnopqrstuvwxyz
B bcdefghijklmnopqrstuvwxyza
C cdefghijklmnopqrstuvwxyzab
D defghijklmnopqrstuvwxyzabc
E efghijklmnopqrstuvwxyzabcd
F fghijklmnopqrstuvwxyzabcde
G ghijklmnopqrstuvwxyzabcdef
H hijklmnopqrstuvwxyzabcdefg
I ijklmnopqrstuvwxyzabcdefgh
J jklmnopqrstuvwxyzabcdefghi
K klmnopqrstuvwxyzabcdefghij
L lmnopqrstuvwxyzabcdefghijk
M mnopqrstuvwxyzabcdefghijkl
N nopqrstuvwxyzabcdefghijklm
O opqrstuvwxyzabcdefghijklmn
P pqrstuvwxyzabcdefghijklmno
```

```
Q  qrstuvwxyzabcdefghijklmnop
R  rstuvwxyzabcdefghijklmnopq
S  stuvwxyzabcdefghijklmnopqr
T  tuvwxyzabcdefghijklmnopqrs
U  uvwxyzabcdefghijklmnopqrst
V  vwxyzabcdefghijklmnopqrstu
W  wxyzabcdefghijklmnopqrstuv
X  xyzabcdefghijklmnopqrstuvw
Y  yzabcdefghijklmnopqrstuvwx
Z  zabcdefghijklmnopqrstuvwxy
```

Both parties need to decide on a secret keyword. This keyword is not written down anywhere, but memorized.

To encode the message, first write down the message:

```
meetmebythetree
```

Then, write the keyword (which in this case is *scones*), repeated as many times as necessary:

```
sconessconessco
meetmebythetree
```

Now you can look up the column *S* in the table and follow it down until it meets the *M* row. The value at the intersection is the letter *e*. All the letters would be thus encoded:

```
sconessconessco
meetmebythetree
egsgqwtahuiljgs
```

The encoded message is now `egsgqwtahuiljgs`.

To decode, the person would use the secret keyword and do the opposite.

Let's get started:

1. At the command prompt, type **cd alphabet-cipher**.

2. Run the tests with `lein test`. If you would like a quicker feedback cycle, you might want to try the lein-test-refresh plug-in (*http://bit.ly/lein-test-refresh*). It allows you to continually run tests every time the file is changed.

3. Make the tests pass.

The source code can be found in *src/alphabet_cipher/coder.clj*:

```
(ns alphabet-cipher.coder)

(defn encode [keyword message]
  "encodeme")
```

```
(defn decode [keyword message]
  "decodeme")
```

The test code can be found in *test/alphabet_cipher/coder_test.clj*:

```
(ns alphabet-cipher.coder-test
  (:require [clojure.test :refer :all]
            [alphabet-cipher.coder :refer :all]))

(deftest test-encode
  (testing "can encode given a secret keyword"
    (is (= "hmkbxebpxpmyllyrxiiqtoltfgzzv"
           (encode "vigilance" "meetmeontuesdayeveningatseven")))
    (is (= "egsgqwtahuiljgs"
           (encode "scones" "meetmebythetree")))))

(deftest test-decode
  (testing "can decode an cyrpted message given a secret keyword"
    (is (= "meetmeontuesdayeveningatseven"
           (decode "vigilance" "hmkbxebpxpmyllyrxiiqtoltfgzzv")))
    (is (= "meetmebythetree"
           (decode "scones" "egsgqwtahuiljgs")))))
```

Today, get the **test-encode** test passing.

Day 2

Continue working on the *Alphabet Cipher* kata.

Today, complete the exercise by getting the **test-decode** test passing.

Day 3

Today we are going to do the *Wonderland Number* kata.

Wonderland is a strange place. There is a wonderland number that is also quite strange.

You must find a way to generate this wonderland number:

- It has six digits.
- If you multiply it by 2, 3, 4, 5, or 6, the resulting number has all the same digits as the original number. The only difference is the position that they are in.

To get started on this kata:

1. At the command prompt, type **cd wonderland-number**.
2. Run the tests with **lein test**.
3. Make the tests pass!

The source file is in *src/wonderland_number/finder.clj*:

```
(ns wonderland-number.finder)

(defn wonderland-number []
  ;; calculate me
  42)
```

The test file is in *test/wonderland_number/finder_test.clj*:

```
(ns wonderland-number.finder-test
  (:require [clojure.test :refer :all]
            [wonderland-number.finder :refer :all]))

(defn hasAllTheSameDigits? [n1 n2]
  (let [s1 (set (str n1))
        s2 (set (str n2))]
    (= s1 s2)))

(deftest test-wonderland-number
  (testing "A wonderland number must have the following things true about it"
    (let [wondernum (wonderland-number)]
      (is (= 6 (count (str (wonderland-number)))))
      (is (hasAllTheSameDigits? wondernum (* 2 wondernum)))
      (is (hasAllTheSameDigits? wondernum (* 3 wondernum)))
      (is (hasAllTheSameDigits? wondernum (* 4 wondernum)))
      (is (hasAllTheSameDigits? wondernum (* 5 wondernum)))
      (is (hasAllTheSameDigits? wondernum (* 6 wondernum))))))
```

Day 4

Continue on with the *Wonderland Number* kata. If you have finished the exercise early, you might think of finding other special numbers. For example, what about numbers under 1,000 that are equal to *the sum of the cubes of its digits*?

Day 5

Today is a fun one. We are going to do the *Fox, Goose, and Bag of Corn* kata.

One of Lewis Carroll's favorite puzzles to ask children was the one about the *Fox, Goose, and Bag of Corn*. It has to do with getting them all safely across a river.

The rules for this puzzle are:

- You must get the fox, goose, and bag of corn safely across to the other side of the river.
- You can only carry one item on the boat across with you.
- The fox cannot be left alone with the goose (or it will be eaten).
- The goose cannot be left alone with the corn (or it will be eaten).

The data structure to represent this puzzle is a vector of vectors.

The starting position is you, the fox, the goose, and corn on one side of the river. The boat is empty. The other river bank is empty:

```
[[[:fox :goose :corn :you] [:boat] []]]
```

You could take the corn on the boat with you:

```
[[[:fox :goose :corn :you] [:boat] []]
 [[:fox :goose] [:boat :corn :you] []]]
```

But then the fox would eat the goose!

The goal is to have the plan in steps so that all make it safely to the other side:

```
[[[:fox :goose :corn :you] [:boat] []]
 ...
 [[[] [:boat] [:fox :goose :corn :you]]]]
```

Let's begin:

1. At the command prompt, type **cd fox-goose-bag-of-corn**.

2. Run the tests with lein test.

3. Make the tests pass!

The source file is in *src/fox_goose_bag_of_corn/puzzle.clj*:

```clojure
(ns fox-goose-bag-of-corn.puzzle)

(def start-pos [[[:fox :goose :corn :you] [:boat] []]])

(defn river-crossing-plan []
  start-pos)
```

The test file is in *test/fox_goose_bag_of_corn/puzzle_test.clj*:

```clojure
(ns fox-goose-bag-of-corn.puzzle-test
  (:require [clojure.test :refer :all]
            [fox-goose-bag-of-corn.puzzle :refer :all]
            [clojure.set]))

(defn validate-move [step1 step2]
  (testing "only you and another thing can move"
    (let [diff1 (clojure.set/difference step1 step2)
          diff2 (clojure.set/difference step2 step1)
          diffs (concat diff1 diff2)
          diff-num (count diffs)]
      (is (> 3 diff-num))
      (when (pos? diff-num)
        (is (contains? (set diffs) :you)))
      step2)))
```

```
(deftest test-river-crossing-plan
  (let [crossing-plan (map (partial map set) (river-crossing-plan))]
    (testing "you begin with the fox, goose and corn on one side of the river"
      (is (= [#{:you :fox :goose :corn} #{:boat} #{}]
             (first crossing-plan))))
    (testing "you end with the fox, goose and corn on one side of the river"
      (is (= [#{} #{:boat} #{:you :fox :goose :corn}]
             (last crossing-plan))))
    (testing "things are safe"
      (let [left-bank (map first crossing-plan)
            right-bank (map last crossing-plan)]
        (testing "the fox and the goose should never be left alone together"
          (is (empty?
               (filter #(= % #{:fox :goose}) (concat left-bank right-bank)))))
        (testing "the goose and the corn should never be left alone together"
          (is (empty?
               (filter #(= % #{:goose :corn}) (concat left-bank right-bank)))))))
    (testing "The boat can carry only you plus one other"
      (let [boat-positions (map second crossing-plan)]
        (is (empty?
             (filter #(> (count %) 3) boat-positions)))))
    (testing "moves are valid"
      (let [left-moves (map first crossing-plan)
            middle-moves (map second crossing-plan)
            right-moves (map last crossing-plan)]
        (reduce validate-move left-moves)
        (reduce validate-move middle-moves)
        (reduce validate-move right-moves )))))
```

Week 5

We are going be be continuing on with our Wonderland Clojure katas.

Day 1

Last week we started the *Fox, Goose, and Bag of Corn* kata. Take today to finish working on it. If you have already finished, take a look at Core Logic (*https://github.com/clojure/core.logic*) library to see if you can solve it in a different way.

Day 2

We are going to continue with the *Doublets* kata.

This Clojure kata comes from *Alice in Wonderland*'s author, Lewis Carroll. He came up with this word puzzle that he named *Doublets*.

The puzzle is to take two words of the same length and find a way of linking the first word to the second word by only changing one letter at a time. At the end of the transformation, there will be a collection of words that show the beginning word being changed into the ending word, one letter at a time. All the *word links* must be in Lewis Carroll's own words:

> …it is de rigueur that the links should be English words, such as might be used in good society.

> —Lewis Carroll

Also the word links should be words that are found in the dictionary. No proper nouns.

Here are some examples.

The Doublet of DOOR to LOCK is:

```
door
boor
book
look
lock
```

The Doublet of BANK to LOAN is:

```
bank
bonk
book
look
loon
loan
```

The Doublet of WHEAT into BREAD is:

```
wheat
cheat
cheap
cheep
creep
creed
breed
bread
```

To get started:

- At the command prompt, type **cd doublets**.
- Run the tests with **lein test**.
- Make the tests pass!

A sample dictionary has been included with a few words to get things going. After you solve the kata, you might want to try a bigger dictionary to discover more exciting doublets.

This kata is a bit tricky. It might take you some time to solve it. One hint is to start with a really tiny dictionary at first, just a few words. You might also take a look at the clojure function `tree-seq` (although there are many other ways to solve this).

The source file to get your started is in *src/doublets/solver.clj*:

```clojure
(ns doublets.solver
  (:require [clojure.java.io :as io]
            [clojure.edn :as edn]))

(def words (-> "words.edn"
               (io/resource)
               (slurp)
               (read-string)))

(defn doublets [word1 word2]
  "make me work")
```

The test file is located in *src/doublets/solver_test.clj*:

```clojure
(ns doublets.solver-test
  (:require [clojure.test :refer :all]
            [doublets.solver :refer :all]))

(deftest solver-test
  (testing "with word links found"
    (is (= ["head" "heal" "teal" "tell" "tall" "tail"]
           (doublets "head" "tail")))

    (is (= ["door" "boor" "book" "look" "lock"]
           (doublets "door" "lock")))

    (is (= ["bank" "bonk" "book" "look" "loon" "loan"]
           (doublets "bank" "loan")))

    (is (= ["wheat" "cheat" "cheap" "cheep" "creep" "creed" "breed" "bread"]
           (doublets "wheat" "bread"))))

  (testing "with no word links found"
    (is (= []
           (doublets "ye" "freezer")))))
```

Day 3

Continue on with the *Doublets* kata. If you have finished, try expanding the dictionary and discovering some other doublets.

Day 4

Today's kata is *Magic Square*.

This puzzle comes from Lewis Carroll. The magic part is when the values on a square are arranged so that adding them up in any direction results in a constant sum.

You have the following values:

```
1.0
1.5
2.0
2.5
3.0
3.5
4.0
4.5
5.0
```

You need to arrange them in a 3 x 3 matrix so that:

- The sums of numbers in each row = magic number
- The sums of numbers in each column = magic number
- The sums of numbers in each diagonal = magic number

To get started:

1. At the command prompt, type **cd magic-square**.
2. Run the tests with `lein test`.
3. Make the tests pass!

The source code is in *src/magic_square/puzzle.clj*:

```clojure
(ns magic-square.puzzle)

(def values [1.0 1.5 2.0 2.5 3.0 3.5 4.0 4.5 5.0])

(defn magic-square [values]
  [[1.0 1.5 2.0]
   [2.5 3.0 3.5]
   [4.0 4.5 5.0]])
```

The test code is in *test/magic_square/puzzle_test.clj*:

```clojure
(ns magic-square.puzzle-test
  (:require [clojure.test :refer :all]
            [magic-square.puzzle :refer :all]))

(defn sum-rows [m]
```

```
    (map #(reduce + %) m))

(defn sum-cols [m]
  [(reduce + (map first m))
   (reduce + (map second m))
   (reduce + (map last m))])

(defn sum-diagonals [m]
  [(+ (get-in m [0 0]) (get-in m [1 1]) (get-in m [2 2]))
   (+ (get-in m [2 0]) (get-in m [1 1]) (get-in m [0 2]))])

(deftest test-magic-square
  (testing "all the rows, columns, and diagonal add to the same number"
    (is (= (set (sum-rows (magic-square values)))
           (set (sum-cols (magic-square values)))
           (set (sum-diagonals (magic-square values)))))))
```

Day 5

More *Magic Square* kata. If you have finished already, try exploring what a 4x4 magic square would look like.

Week 6

This is our last week working the *Wonderland Clojure* katas, so have fun and enjoy.

Day 1

Today is a maze kata called *Tiny Maze*.

Alice found herself very tiny and wandering around Wonderland. Even the grass around her seemed like a maze.

This is a tiny maze solver.

A maze is represented by a matrix:

```
[[:S 0 1]
 [1  0 1]
 [1  0 :E]]
```

- *S* is the start of the maze
- *E* is the end of the maze
- *1* is a wall that you cannot pass through
- *0* is a free space that you can move through

The goal is to get to the end of the maze. A solved maze will have an *:x* in the start, the path, and the end of the maze, like this:

```
[[:x :x 1]
 [1  :x 1]
 [1  :x :x]]
```

To get started:

1. At the command prompt, type **cd tiny-maze**.

2. Run the tests with `lein test`.

3. Make the tests pass!

The source code is in *src/tiny_maze/solver.clj*:

```
(ns tiny-maze.solver)

(defn solve-maze [maze])
```

The test code is in *test/tiny_maze/solver_test.clj*:

```
(ns tiny-maze.solver-test
  (:require [clojure.test :refer :all]
            [tiny-maze.solver :refer :all]))

(deftest test-solve-maze
  (testing "can find way to exit with 3x3 maze"
    (let [maze [[:S 0 1]
                [1  0 1]
                [1  0 :E]]
          sol [[:x :x 1]
               [1  :x 1]
               [1  :x :x]]]
      (is (= sol (solve-maze maze)))))

  (testing "can find way to exit with 4x4 maze"
    (let [maze [[:S 0 0 1]
                [1  1 0 0]
                [1  0 0 1]
                [1  1 0 :E]]
          sol [[:x :x :x 1]
               [1  1 :x 0]
               [1  0 :x 1]
               [1  1 :x :x]]]
      (is (= sol (solve-maze maze)))))))
```

Day 2

Continue with the *Tiny Maze* kata. If you are done, can you make the maze bigger?

Day 3

Because Alice ended up having trouble with cards, our final kata is the *Card Game of War* kata.

This kata is a version of the classic card game (War (*http://bit.ly/war_crd_game*)).

The rules of this card game are quite simple:

- There are two players.
- The cards are all dealt equally to each player.
- Each round, player 1 lays a card down face up at the same time that player 2 lays a card down face up. Whoever has the highest value card wins the round and takes both cards.
- The winning cards are added to the bottom of the winner's deck.
- Aces are high.
- If both cards are of equal value, then the winner is decided upon by the highest suit. The suits ranks in order of ascending value are spades, clubs, diamonds, and hearts.
- The player that runs out of cards loses.
- If both players run out of cards at the same time, it is a draw.

Getting started on this one:

1. At the command prompt, type **cd card-game-war**.
2. Run the tests with **lein test**.
3. In this kata, you will be prompted to fill in your own tests.
4. Make the tests pass!

The source code is in *src/card_game_war/game.clj*:

```clojure
(ns card-game-war.game)

;; feel free to use these cards or use your own data structure
(def suits [:spade :club :diamond :heart])
(def ranks [2 3 4 5 6 7 8 9 10 :jack :queen :king :ace])
(def cards
  (for [suit suits
        rank ranks]
    [suit rank]))

(defn play-round [player1-card player2-card])

(defn play-game [player1-cards player2-cards])
```

The test file is a bit different than in previous exercises. This time, only the descriptions have been provided. It is up to you to write the tests. This will give you freedom in how you want to implement the game and card structures.

```
;; fill in  tests for your game
(deftest test-play-round
  (testing "the highest rank wins the cards in the round"
    ;; this is only here to give you a failing test to start out with
    (is (= 0 1)))
  (testing "queens are higer rank than jacks")
  (testing "kings are higer rank than queens")
  (testing "aces are higer rank than kings")
  (testing "if the ranks are equal, clubs beat spades")
  (testing "if the ranks are equal, diamonds beat clubs")
  (testing "if the ranks are equal, hearts beat diamonds"))

(deftest test-play-game
  (testing "the player loses when they run out of cards")
  (testing "if both players run out of cards then it is a draw"))
```

Day 4

Keep working with the *Card Game of War* kata.

Day 5

This is an extra day to finish up the *Card Game of War* kata. If you have already finished up, you might think about some game changes. What if the round was played with three cards face down and the fourth face up? The value of the face up card takes *all* the cards in the round. Or what if you introduced a random element? Instead of the winner placing the cards at the bottom of her deck, what if the cards were placed randomly in the deck?

Week 7

You made it to the last week!

This week you are going to make your very own web application and deploy it to Heroku (*https://dashboard.heroku.com/apps*), which does web app hosting for Clojure apps. It also offers a nice, free version of hosting that will be perfect for your exercise.

Before you dive into creating your own web application, we will walk through how to set up one to deploy to Heroku. We will take the *cheshire-cat* web application that we created back in Chapter 7 and deploy it to the hosted enviornment.

Day 1

The first thing you will need to do is create an account on Heroku. It is free of charge. You can create your login at *https://signup.heroku.com/dc*.

Next, you will need the *Heroku Toolbelt*. This gives you a nice command-line tool to configure and deploy applications. You can download it from *http://bit.ly/getstar ted_on_heroku*.

Once you have downloaded the tool, you will need to configure it with your username and password. You can do this at the command line by typing **heroku login**. You will be prompted for your email and password:

```
-> heroku login
Enter your Heroku credentials.
Email:
Password:
```

Now you are all set to configure your project.

Go ahead and find the *cheshire-cat* project from Chapter 7, and cd into the root of it.

If you haven't initialized it yet as a Git repo, do so:

```
git init
```

The next step is to create an app on Heroku for it. This will get Heroku ready to receive your code for deployment. Type **heroku create** into your command prompt at the root of the *cheshire-cat* project. You will see:

```
-> heroku create
Creating calm-reaches-2803... done, stack is cedar-14
https://calm-reaches-2803.herokuapp.com/ | ....
Git remote heroku added
```

It created a random application name for you, which you can rename later through the console. It also added a repository called *heroku* to your git config. Once you push your code here, it will automatically deploy.

You need to add a couple configuration changes to your project before you can push your code. This first one is adding an extra dependency to your *project.clj* file. You need to add *javax.servlet/servlet-api* as a dependency.

Go ahead and add it to your *project.clj* file:

```
(defproject cheshire-cat "0.1.0-SNAPSHOT"
  :description "FIXME: write description"
  :url "http://example.com/FIXME"
  :min-lein-version "2.0.0"
  :dependencies [[org.clojure/clojure "1.6.0"]
                 [compojure "1.1.9"]
                 [ring/ring-json "0.3.1"]
                 [org.clojure/clojurescript "0.0-2371"]
                 [cljs-http "0.1.18"]
                 [org.clojure/core.async "0.1.346.0-17112a-alpha"]
                 [enfocus "2.1.0"]
                 [javax.servlet/servlet-api "2.5"]] ❶
  :plugins [[lein-ring "0.8.12"]
```

```
            [lein-cljsbuild "1.0.3"]]
 :ring {:handler cheshire-cat.handler/app}
 :profiles
 {:dev {:dependencies [[javax.servlet/servlet-api "2.5"]
                       [ring-mock "0.1.5"]]}}

 :cljsbuild {
   :builds [{
       :source-paths ["src-cljs"]
       :compiler {
         :output-to "resources/public/main.js"
         :optimizations :whitespace
         :pretty-print true}}]})
```

❶ Add `javax.servlet` to your regular dependencies.

Next, you need to add a *Procfile*. This file controls how Heroku starts up your app.

Create a file in the root of the directory, called *Procfile*. Edit the contents to be:

```
web: lein ring server-headless
```

This will tell Heroku to start up your web application in headless mode (won't open a browser like `lein ring server` does).

You are just about ready to deploy. You will need to commit your all changes with Git. Type in the following:

```
git add .
```

and then:

```
git commit -m "ready for deploy"
```

Finally, you will push them to the Heroku repo for automatic deploy. Enter **git push heroku master**. You will see something like this:

```
-> git push heroku master
Counting objects: 3, done.
Delta compression using up to 8 threads.
Compressing objects: 100% (2/2), done.
Writing objects: 100% (2/2), 226 bytes | 0 bytes/s, done.
Total 2 (delta 1), reused 0 (delta 0)
remote: Compressing source files... done.
remote: Building source:
...
remote: -----> Launching... done, v4
remote:        https://calm-reaches-2803.herokuapp.com/ deployed to Heroku ❶
remote:
remote: Verifying deploy... done.
To https://git.heroku.com/calm-reaches-2803.git
   7386259..ac77a3f  master -> master
```

❶ The app name where it was deployed.

When it is done deploying, you can visit the app name where it was deployed. In this case, it is *https://calm-reaches-2803.herokuapp.com/*. This means you can visit your fading cat web page and see it smile. Open the following link in your browser:

```
https://calm-reaches-2803.herokuapp.com/cat.html
```

Your web application is deployed and hosted on Heroku.

So to review, because you have already created your Heroku account, these are the steps that you will need to do to deploy the web app you will create to Heroku:

1. In your project directory, create your heroku app with **heroku create**.

2. Make sure you have [`javax.servlet/servlet-api "2.5"`] in your application.

3. Create a Procfile in the root of the project with the contents `web: lein ring server-headless`.

4. Commit your changes with Git.

5. Deploy it to Heroku with **git push heroku master**.

6. Your app shoud be live at the Heroku app link.

You are now ready for the week.

Day 2

Today is hammock day. No coding, just thinking. Get some ideas together about what kind of web app you would like to build.

A good suggestion to get you going is first to brainstorm some different ideas on paper. Then get a cup of tea, take another look at your options, and choose which one you like best.

Once you have your idea, draw out what you want your app to look like. Don't forgot to keep it simple!

Day 3

Build your app server. What routes are you going to need? Are you going to do JSON?

Useful areas for review:

- "Creating a Web Server with Compojure" on page 111
- "Using JSON with the Cheshire Library and Ring" on page 115

Day 4

Build your frontend. If you need ClojureScript, it is there for you.

Useful areas for review:

- "Using Clojure in Your Browser with ClojureScript" on page 120
- "Making HTTP Calls with ClojureScript and cljs-http" on page 127
- "DOM Control with ClojureScript and Enfocus" on page 129
- "Event Handling with Enfocus" on page 131
- "Other Useful Web Development Libraries" on page 135

Day 5

Deploy it to Heroku and share it with the world!

Congratulations

You have completed the *Living Clojure* Training Plan!

Your brain is now well adjusted to thinking the functional way and you have all the resources you need to be part of the Clojure community.

I hope you have enjoyed our Clojure journey together. I look forward to your continued success in *living* Clojure.

CHAPTER 11

Further Adventures

The focus of this book has been on the core and most important parts of Clojure that you will need to know to get you going. This was done to ease the cognitive load in learning a new way of thinking. But there is so much more to explore and learn. Clojure is a rich ecosystem with many beautiful areas behind every corner. In this chapter, we are going to mention some suggested areas to explore.

The first area to look at is where Clojure as a language is headed. As this book is being written, *Clojure 1.7* is getting ready to be released. One of the innovations it will bring, is a new fundamental concept called *transducers*.

Get Ready for Transducers

Transducers are a way of decoupling transformations from the data structures. One advantage to this decoupling is that these transformations can be reused and composed. Transducers are bit hard to explain in words, so let's see them in action. We will be using a simple example from *Alice in Wonderland* to illustrate them. We will be taking a collection of transformations to make words acceptable to be in the Queen of Hearts garden.

The first thing we need to do is create a new project and grab the latest version of Clojure 1.7 as well as *core.async*, which we will be also using.

At a command prompt, type the following:

```
lein new queen-of-hearts
```

Next, go ahead a open the *project.clj* page and edit it so that you have the following dependencies:

```
(defproject queen-of-hearts "0.1.0-SNAPSHOT"
  :description "FIXME: write description"
```

```
    :url "http://example.com/FIXME"
    :license {:name "Eclipse Public License"
              :url "http://www.eclipse.org/legal/epl-v10.html"}
    :dependencies [[org.clojure/clojure "1.7.0-alpha4"]
                   [org.clojure/core.async "0.1.346.0-17112a-alpha"]]])
```

Open up the *src/queen_of_hearts/core.clj* file and add *core.async* to the namespace. Also go ahead and get a REPL going:

```
(ns queen-of-hearts.core
  (:require [clojure.core.async :as async]))
```

The next thing we need are some flowers for the queen's garden. Here is a vector with assorted flowers and colors:

```
(def flowers ["white carnation"
              "yellow daffodil"
              "yellow rose"
              "red rose"
              "white rose"
              "purple lily"
              "pink carnation"])
;; -> #'user/flowers
```

The first transformation that the queen is going to insist on is that all the flowers must be red. So we will create a function that will change the color of each flower string to red. We will call it `paint-it-red`. It will simply take the color part of the string and replace it with "red":

```
(defn paint-it-red [s]
  (str "red "
       (last (clojure.string/split s #"\s"))))
```

It takes a white carnation and changes it to be red:

```
(paint-it-red "white carnation")
;; -> "red carnation"
```

We can also try this out mapped across all the flowers:

```
(map paint-it-red flowers)
;; -> ("red carnation"
;;     "red daffodil"
;;     "red rose"
;;     "red rose"
;;     "red rose"
;;     "red lily"
;;     "red carnation")
```

Now that all the flowers are red, we know that the queen only allows roses. All the other flowers must go. We can do this by defining an `is-a-rose?` function and using a filter:

```
(defn is-a-rose? [s]
  (= "rose"
     (last (clojure.string/split s #"\s"))))

(is-a-rose? "yellow rose")
;; -> true
```

We can try it out on the original flowers structure, too:

```
(filter is-a-rose? flowers)
;; -> ("yellow rose" "red rose" "white rose")
```

It works just fine, only the roses are left.

Now here is where the *transducers* come in. We have two transformations that we can apply to a vector of flower strings. In the previous version of Clojure, you would need a data structure to use with map. Not any more.

We can decouple the transformation from the data structure by leaving it off. It returns a *transducer* now:

```
(map paint-it-red)
;; -> #<core$map$fn__4507 clojure.core$map$fn__4507@5c808a3a>
```

The same goes for our filter function:

```
(filter is-a-rose?)
;; -> #<core$filter$fn__4534 clojure.core$filter$fn__4534@54e7453c>
```

We can then take these transducers and describe and compose our transformation for the Queen of Hearts, without the data being present. We can do this with a simple comp form:

```
(def fix-for-the-queen-xform
  (comp
    (map paint-it-red)
    (filter is-a-rose?)))
```

We can run the transformation of the transducers against the data in a few ways:

- We can use *into*, which is a nonlazy way to turn the transformation into a collection.
- We can use *sequence*, which is a lazy way to turn the transformation into a collection.
- We can use *transduce*, which acts like reduce on all the transformed elements.
- We can use *core.async* channels to do the transformations.

Let's look at our flowers examples for each one of these ways.

into takes a transducer and collection to work on and returns the vector we asked for:

```
(into [] fix-for-the-queen-xform flowers)
;; -> ["red rose" "red rose" "red rose"]
```

Sequence takes similar arguments, but as promised, returns a lazy sequence that we can interact with:

```
(class (sequence fix-for-the-queen-xform flowers))
;; -> clojure.lang.LazyTransformer

(take 1 (sequence fix-for-the-queen-xform flowers))
;; -> ("red rose")
```

If we want to finally arrange all our sentences in the vectors into one string, we would use reduce. The way to do this with transducers is to use transduce. It takes a function of two arguments to perform the reduce, as well as an initial data input:

```
(transduce fix-for-the-queen-xform    ❶
           (completing #(str %1 %2 ":")) ❷
           "" ❸
           flowers) ❹
;; -> "red rose:red rose:red rose:"
```

❶ The first argument is our transducer xform.

❷ The next argument is the reducing function. It needs a function that is a two-arg function, just like the one used in a reduce. We need to surround it with a *completing* function to add a suitable one-arg function for it too, that the transducer needs.

❸ The empty string is our initial data for the reducing function.

❹ Finally, add the data.

One advantage of using transducers is that we can reuse the transformation with other things, like *core.async*.

Core.async has a really nice way to define channels with a transducer that will transform each element on the channel:

```
(def flower-chan (async/chan 1 fix-for-the-queen-xform))
```

Let's define another channel to reduce the results of the flower-chan to a string:

```
(def result-chan (async/reduce
                   (completing #(str %1 %2 ":"))
                   ""
                   flower-chan))
```

Finally, let's actually put the flower data onto the flower-chan and let the data transformations flow:

```
(async/onto-chan flower-chan flowers)
;; -> #<ManyToManyChannel ... >
```

At last, we can get our result off the result channel and revel in the beauty of asynchronous data transducers:

```
(def flowers-for-the-queen (async/<!! result-chan))

flowers-for-the-queen
;; -> "red rose:red rose:red rose:"
```

This is just a small taste of the *transducers* coming to Clojure soon. The decoupling of data from transformations will allow for simpler and more reusable code. You have many adventures with them ahead of you.

In addition to the areas to explore in web application development and transducers, there are quite of few great books and papers that you might want to explore.

Further Reading

The list of suggested further reading is by no means exhaustive, but it certainly is a good start:

- *Alice in Wonderland* by Lewis Carroll
- *The Joy of Clojure* by Michael Fogus and Chris Houser (Manning Publications)
- *Mastering Clojure Macros* by Colin Jones (The Pragmatic Programmers)
- *The Little Schemer* by Daniel P. Friedman and Matthias Felleisen (MIT Press)
- *The Hunting of the Snark* by Lewis Carroll
- *ClojureScript Up and Running* by Stuart Sierra and Luke VanderHart (O'Reilly)
- Recursive Functions of Symbolic Expressions and their Computation by Machine, Part I (*http://bit.ly/mccarthy_recursive*) by John McCarthy (MIT 1960)

Welcome again to the Clojure community. You have many adventures in store for you in the wonderful world of Clojure.

Index

About the Author

Carin Meier started off as a professional ballet dancer, studied physics in college, and has been developing software for both the enterprise and entrepreneur ever since. She has a strong background in Ruby and Clojure. She is highly involved in the community and has spoken at many conferences, including keynoting at OSCON and Strange Loop. She also helps lead the Cincinnati Functional Programmers group.

Colophon

The animal on the cover of *Living Clojure* is a water rail (*Railus aquaticus*), a species of bird found breeding in wetlands from the British Isles to Asia. With the African and Madagascan rails it constitutes a superspecies that likely evolved originally in the New World.

The water rail can be very elusive outside of nocturnal migrations, confining itself to the wetland terrain where a narrow body and long legs allow it to deftly negotiate long, tangled grasses; its facility on the ground also renders flying and swimming secondary modes of transport. Often more evident by its vocalizations than by sight, the water rail uses a piglike grunting and squealing called *sharming* to mark a particular territory. Fierce territoriality characterizes the bird's behaviors both in the breeding and winter feeding seasons.

Within the densely grown patches of marshland over which they demonstrate a fierce territoriality, a monogamous pair of water rails—for the breeding season, at least—mix ongoing courtship calls and displays with the tedium of nest-building, incubation, and feeding. Both parents share the task of incubating eggs within nests built near the water level. Chicks covered in black down develop quickly and follow parents out of the nest mere hours after hatching.

Water rails are opportunistic omnivores with a wide range of means for obtaining sustenance. A bird of the species will deviate from well-worn paths to food through thick reedbeds and marshes to pluck berries from a bush or pick at carrion. It is also capable of discrete aggresion, drowning small animals it has trapped or using its long beak to impale others when necessary.

The cover image is from *The Elements of Ornithology*. The cover fonts are URW Typewriter and Guardian Sans. The text font is Adobe Minion Pro; the heading font is Adobe Myriad Condensed; and the code font is Dalton Maag's Ubuntu Mono.

Have it your way.

Get even more for your money.

Join the O'Reilly Community, and register the O'Reilly books you own. It's free, and you'll get:

- $4.99 ebook upgrade offer
- 40% upgrade offer on O'Reilly print books
- Membership discounts on books and events
- Free lifetime updates to ebooks and videos
- Multiple ebook formats, DRM FREE
- Participation in the O'Reilly community
- Newsletters
- Account management
- 100% Satisfaction Guarantee

Signing up is easy:

1. Go to: oreilly.com/go/register
2. Create an O'Reilly login.
3. Provide your address.
4. Register your books.

Note: English-language books only

To order books online:
oreilly.com/store

For questions about products or an order:
orders@oreilly.com

To sign up to get topic-specific email announcements and/or news about upcoming books, conferences, special offers, and new technologies:
elists@oreilly.com

For technical questions about book content:
booktech@oreilly.com

To submit new book proposals to our editors:
proposals@oreilly.com

O'Reilly books are available in multiple DRM-free ebook formats. For more information:
oreilly.com/ebooks

O'REILLY®

Milton Keynes UK
Ingram Content Group UK Ltd.
UKHW030225300324
440266UK00009B/489